Creating Successful Inclusion Programs

Guidelines for Teachers and Administrators

P. 58
belonging
mastery
independence
generosity

Martin Henley

empowerment
belonging
co-operation

National Educational Service

Cover art and design by Grannan Graphic Design, Ltd.

Text design by T.G. Design Group

Printed in the United States of America

ISBN: 1-932127-17-8

Dedication

For Arlene

Who always asks, "Are you writing?"

Table of Contents

Introduction

IN THE UTOPIAN SOCIETY fictionalized in his book *Brave New World*, Aldous Huxley's populace is separated at birth into categories of Alphas, Betas, Deltas, and Epsilons. Each classification delegates duties and honors to citizens in descending alphabetical order; the Alphas rule and the Epsilons clean up. Our schools share a similar penchant for categorization and separation based on ability. In Huxley's novel, people are segregated to make their world a more orderly place. The educational rationale for categorizing and separating students is to meet individual needs. The principle of meeting educational needs is a worthwhile goal that is embedded in federal law, but so is integration of students with their non-disabled peers.

From 1999 to 2000, most students with disabilities spent the majority of their school day in the regular classroom. Others were educated primarily in special education classrooms. Students with specific learning disabilities and speech impairments spent the most time in regular classrooms. But only 3.2% of students with mental retardation, 4.5% of students with emotional disturbance, and .5% of students with autism were educated alongside their non-disabled peers (U.S. Department of Education, 2002). Those who required social development the most had the least access to normal school experiences.

If the practice of segregating students by disability showed some success, at least the ends would justify the means, but signs of success are meager. A nationwide survey of "blue ribbon" programs for students with emotional disabilities found an overwhelming emphasis on behavior control and scant attention paid to educational needs (Knitzer, Steinberg, & Fleisch, 1990). The results are predictable. Approximately 50% of students with emotional and behavioral problems drop out of school (U.S. Department of Education, 2000); these forgotten young people are America's Epsilons. The time is ripe for change.

WHAT IS INCLUSION?

Inclusion is a federal mandate to provide special education services in the regular classroom, and the final stage in a steady progression of civil and educational rights for individuals with disabilities. It was not so long ago that the presence of a disability put a youngster on the fast track to life in an institution. This tragic practice went into decline in 1975 with the passage of the Individuals with Disabilities Education Act (IDEA). Thanks to this groundbreaking federal law, students with disabilities have the right to a free and appropriate education in public schools. Yet for some students, access to a public school education has been at the expense of a normal school experience because of the widespread separation of students based on disability.

Sometimes students are categorized by disability and placed in separate special education classrooms where they remain until they exit school for good. Other special education students spend part of their day in a regular classroom but are required to leave their classroom for special education tutoring. Separation has fostered a slew of negative consequences. Stereotypes and low expectations abound. The further away from the mainstream of a normal school experience, the higher the likelihood a student will fail. For every minute of special education instruction students receive, they lose a minute of regular classroom instruction.

It is likely that future educators will look back at the inclusion movement and wonder what took so long. In the future, the practice of separating students because of differences in ability might seem as undemocratic as segregation by race, ethnicity, or religion. During my 35-year career in education, I have had the opportunity to work in and visit hundreds of special and regular education classrooms. Throughout this time, I have observed a simple but dynamic principle: good teachers are equally effective with both regular and special education students. Make no mistake, the work of teaching students with diverse abilities is difficult. Without proper administrative support, even the best teacher can lose heart.

Within this book, I have recorded teaching and administrative qualities that characterize successful inclusion programs. Much of this information is derived from research, and an equal amount is based on my experience as an educator. Throughout, the emphasis is on practical strategies for organizing and implementing inclusion programs.

This book is written for administrators, teachers, and parents who believe that for many students with disabilities, the regular classroom is the appropriate educational placement. **Chapter 1** explains the meaning of inclusion and why it is a growing trend. **Chapter 2** describes some of the history behind the inclusion movement and the passing of the Individuals with Disabilities Education Act (IDEA). **Chapter 3** delves into the legal requirements of federal and state law. **Chapter 4** explains the organizational dynamics of successful inclusion programs. **Chapter 5** identifies teaching strategies that have been proven effective within inclusion programs, and **Chapter 6** explains how to deal with discipline and problem behaviors in an inclusive setting. **Chapter 7** wraps up with a discussion of how inclusion programs benefit the entire education system.

Chapter 1

Inclusion Can Work

THIS BOOK IS ABOUT INCLUSION, a controversial shift in how students with disabilities are educated. Inclusion bridges the gap between regular and special education by minimizing the practice of separating students for special education instruction. Within inclusive classrooms, students with disabilities learn side by side with their non-disabled peers.

In the past, special educators were primarily responsible for providing special education; within inclusion programs, regular education teachers share that responsibility. Proponents of inclusion regard the movement as a logical continuation of the decades-long struggle to integrate individuals with disabilities into the mainstream of public school life. Others fear that regular education teachers are not suitably trained to provide appropriate individualized education to students with disabilities.

Inclusion is not for every student. The Individuals with Disabilities Education Act (IDEA) requires that students with special needs be educated in the "least restrictive environment." Least restrictive is a relative, not an absolute, term. Every school system is mandated by law to offer a variety of special education placements, ranging from full-time regular classroom placement (inclusion, the least restrictive) to residential placement (the most restrictive). In between least and most restrictive exist a variety of options including pull-out programs for special education tutoring (the student spends the majority of time in the regular classroom), special education classrooms (self-contained classes populated only by students with special needs), and alternative schools (private or public school programs). The decision to place a student in an inclusion classroom is made when a student's family and school officials meet to design the student's individual education program (IEP).

THE INCLUSION MOVEMENT

Several sources have spurred the inclusion movement. The federal special education law Individuals with Disabilities Education Act (IDEA) requires that the regular classroom be the first consideration when deciding on an appropriate special education placement. Many parents and advocates for students with disabilities argue that inclusion in school is the best preparation for inclusion in the community. In addition, a study by Baker, Wang, and Walberg (1994) reported that special education students perform better academically within the regular classroom, rather than in special education classrooms. Furthermore, many special education students express a preference for regular classroom instruction.

Some educators believe that inclusion saves money. The more time special education students spend in the regular classroom, the reasoning goes, the less need for special education teachers, supervisors, and administrators. The perceived cost-cutting opportunities involved in inclusion present an attractive option to financially strapped school systems. It is true that well-conceived inclusion programs can save money over a period of time, but in most instances, inclusion is more expensive in the short term. Long-term savings come from reduced referrals for special education services, shared materials and resources, decreased out-of-district placements, reduced transportation costs, and a declining need for space to house special education programs. Short-term monetary increases occur because of the need to support regular and special education teachers through in-service training, planning sessions, and professional consultation.

Above and beyond educational considerations, inclusion of individuals with disabilities into the mainstream of American life is a nationwide movement with vast social repercussions. Forty-nine million Americans with disabilities constitute the single largest minority in the country. Individuals with disabilities exceed the combined populations of California, Colorado, Montana, Nevada, New Mexico, Oregon, Utah, and Wyoming, (U.S. Department of Commerce, 1997). Sooner or later, nearly everyone is disabled through age, sickness, or injury. Disabilities are nothing to be ashamed of, nor do they limit an individual's potential. The author John Milton was blind. Composer Ludwig van Beethoven was deaf. George Washington had a learning disability. In more recent times such prominent figures as Henry Ford, Nelson Rockefeller, and Thomas Edison had learning disabilities.

Since the passage of the Individuals with Disabilities Education Act in 1975, individuals with disabilities have made remarkable gains. Yet young people with disabilities still face a stiff challenge in schools. Negative stereotypes, inadequate teacher training, and one-size-fits-all instructional strategies create limitations that are difficult to overcome. Perhaps more than anything else, individuals with disabilities are limited by the psychological and educational terms used to describe them. Consider some of the language used to identify students with disabilities: "handicapped," "mentally retarded," and "emotionally disturbed." These terms, which open the door to special education services by identifying a disability, create stereotypes and imprint a perception of permanent inadequacy that is difficult to overcome. When people with disabilities are queried about their most difficult hurdles, they nearly always mention negative stereotypes that limit their opportunities as a first response (Taylor & Searl, 1987).

A SELF-FULFILLING PROPHECY

Several years ago, I supervised a student teacher who was mentoring in a self-contained class for students with intellectual disabilities. Most of the eight students had Down syndrome, a genetic disorder that at one time put children on the fast track to life in an institution. My visit was on St. Patrick's Day. The school was festooned with green bunting and other Irish paraphernalia. When I entered the classroom, I saw seven of the eight students in odd costumes. The teacher proudly told me that the student teacher had done an excellent Native American unit and the students were going to do a "harvest dance" for me. A chair was placed in the center of the room, and with some urging from the teacher, the students began chanting and dancing around me. One student refused and he was disciplined. I admired the young rebel. Clearly he was embarrassed, as was I, by the way the teachers displayed the children in beads, headbands, and feathers on the same day that all other students were dressed in green. I wondered how this teacher could be so oblivious to the contrast she created between her students and the rest of the school population.

On my way out, the teacher walked me to the parking lot. "It's so hard teaching these students," she said. "Before last Christmas holiday, they knew how to add and subtract two-digit numbers," she continued. "After the holidays, they had forgotten everything!" She paused and then added, "Well, you know how it is with the retarded." She shrugged her shoulders and walked back into the building. Evidently, the idea that perhaps her teaching methods could be improved had not crossed her mind; this is the crux of the dilemma faced by teachers who work with students with special needs. Students need a "label" to get special education services, but the diagnosis can become a self-fulfilling prophecy of ineptitude. Good and Wittrock (2000) define self-fulfilling prophecy as an erroneous expectation that causes the expectation to become true.

Ryan McGovern, a 20-year-old education major, visited a successful inclusion program and discovered that "disabled" does not mean "un-abled."

One special needs student especially moved me. I will call him John. John has cerebral palsy, a disorder that restricts his movement. As most people would, I viewed John, and saw only his wheelchair. Upon further inspection, I discovered a wonderful, creative, and intelligent student who would not allow his disability to slow him down in any way. John knew more about economics than any other student in the room, myself included. I mention this student as an example of stereotyping. I will hold the lesson John taught me forever, [as more memorable] than anything else I learned during my observations.

Ryan's positive experience helped him see John not simply in terms of his disability, but as a complex person with many attributes. Teachers set the stage for success when they believe in their students. Conversely, low teacher expectations establish a handicap that is as difficult to overcome as the disability itself. Rosenthal and Jacobsen (1968) demonstrated that teacher expectations can lead to self-fulfilling prophecies in their classic study, "Pygmalion in the Classroom." The researchers told a group of elementary teachers that specific students were "late bloomers." At the end of the year, these "late bloomers" outpaced peers despite the fact that in reality, the "bloomer" attribute was contrived. The researchers concluded that the selected students received preferential treatment, which accelerated their progress. Further research has demonstrated that teachers' expectations can influence how they interact with students and how the students perform in the classroom (Whittrock, 1986).

THE BENEFITS OF INCLUSION

Inclusion programs have produced numerous positive results for students with disabilities as well as for students who are non-disabled. The following is a summary of research findings:

- Students with physical disabilities achieved individual education plan (IEP) goals more effectively in inclusive classrooms than in separate special education placements (Miller, 1996).

- Students with special needs who are educated in regular education classrooms do better academically and socially than comparable students in non-inclusive settings (Baker, Wang, & Walberg, 1994).

- The academic progress of non-disabled students is not hampered by having students with disabilities in their classrooms (Staub & Peck, 1994).

- Documented benefits for non-disabled students are: 1) tolerance for individual differences, 2) growth in social skills, 3) improved self-concept, and 4) enhanced interpersonal skills (Staub & Peck, 1994).

- Parents have reported positive outcomes for non-disabled children within classes that included students with severe disabilities (Giangreco, Edelman, Cloniger, & Dennis, 1992).

- Students with moderate disabilities demonstrated increased independence and improved functional skills within inclusive classrooms (Janney, Snell, Beers, & Rayners, 1995).

- Included students acquired age-appropriate behaviors, developed friendships and demonstrated increased self-esteem. Students without disabilities were perceived by teachers and parents to have grown in self-esteem and in acceptance of individual differences (Janney, Snell, Beers, & Rayners, 1995).

Inclusion can work, but for every tale of successful inclusion there is a countervailing story of disappointment. It is not enough to simply seat non-disabled students and students with disabilities in a classroom together. Fortunately, there is a comprehensive record of the ingredients that lead to successful inclusion programs. For every struggling student, there is a path to success.

The next chapter provides background on the historical treatment of children with special needs, the legislation leading up to the Individuals with Disabilities Education Act (IDEA), what constitutes a disability, how inclusion programs fit in with the legislation, and a section on frequently asked questions with answers.

Chapter 2

The Quiet Revolution

WHEN I WAS A BOY GROWING UP IN THE 1950s, it was rare to see a person with disabilities in public. My first recollections of individuals with disabilities are of World War II veterans—middle-aged men on crutches, missing a leg, others walking down the street with an empty shirt sleeve doubled up and pinned at the shoulder. One day when I was about 7, I encountered a man with a prosthetic arm. I was intrigued by how he managed to grab items with his apparatus of wire and steel, but I shied away from him because his "hook" looked sinister. If anyone had asked me to describe a person with disabilities at that point in my life, I would have used the word "cripple."

I encountered my first person with a mental disability at age 11. I saw a man walking back and forth in front of a house. He was waving to passing cars and laughing. He frightened me, but he also fascinated me. He shuffled back and forth, never moving more than 20 feet in either direction. He was wearing a shabby brown suit, and I guessed his age at around 30. He waved to me. I waved back and kept walking. I did not look back and I never walked up that street again.

As time went by, I forgot about the laughing man in the brown suit. The cliché "out of sight, out of mind" was an apt description of my attitude. I pitied the occasional person with disabilities that I encountered on the street. Each was an oddity that I thought about as long as it took me to walk by. It wasn't until I enrolled in the Syracuse University graduate program in special education many years later that I considered the struggles faced by individuals with disabilities. My change in attitude began the day I met Burton Blatt.

"Burt," as everyone called him, was the Dean of the School of Education. He was a short, stocky, dynamo of a man. He treated everyone—janitors, secretaries, students, faculty members—with the same unbridled enthusiasm. His vitality was magnetic, and like a lot of other graduate students, I adopted him as my mentor. Burt revered two things in life: truth and action. He was intensely concerned about the second-class status conferred on individuals with disabilities. He believed that the presence of a disability did not diminish an individual's humanity or his or her constitutional rights. Unlike many academics, Burt Blatt was not satisfied with passively studying a problem; he did something about it.

In the fall of 1965, Senator Robert Kennedy visited several institutions for individuals with mental retardation in New York State. He was dismayed at the inhumane conditions he observed, and his widely reported comments shocked the public and angered many state officials, including Governor Rockefeller, who claimed that Kennedy was exaggerating. In characteristic style, Burt decided to find out for himself.

With his friend Fred Kaplan, a professional photographer, Burt got permission to visit several back wards in New York State institutions. Kaplan took hundreds of photographs with a hidden camera he had attached to his belt. In hopes of drawing national attention to the horrendous conditions they observed, Burt Blatt and Fred Kaplan published a photographic account of their experiences in *Christmas in Purgatory* (1966). What follows is a brief detail from their book:

> *You see the children first. An anonymous boy, about 6, squeezes his hand through the opening at the bottom of a locked door and begs, "Touch me. Play with me." A 13-year-old boy lies naked, on his own wastes, in a corner of a solitary-confinement cell. Children, 1 and 2 years old, lie silent in cribs all day, without contact with any adult, without playthings, without any apparent stimulation. The cribs are placed side-by-side and head-to-head to fill every available bit of space in the room. The 6 year old who begged "Touch me" was one of 40 or more unkept children of various ages crawling around a bare floor in a bare room. Their dormitory held about 100 children. It was connected to nine other dormitories containing 900 more.* (p. 39)

While the inhumane treatment of individuals with mental retardation was an atrocity in its own right, Burt's research hardly told the full story. In 1970, Congress estimated that two million children were excluded from public school because of physical, behavioral, or mental deficiencies (Cottle, 1976). The Task Force on Children Out of School (1970) uncovered myriad examples of students denied a normal education because they did not fit the system:

- Harris Williams, aged 10, was placed in a special class for children with mental retardation because he was a "behavior problem." Harris was in the special class for a year before his mother found out.

- Kathy Fitzgerald was 6 years old when her mother tried to enroll her in school. She presented the principal with a medical certificate stating that Kathy's seizure disorder was under control thanks to medication. The principal said that he would not enroll Kathy. After several unsuccessful efforts at public school enrollment, Mrs. Fitzgerald was able to get Kathy admitted to a private school for "crippled children."

In 1919, Supreme Court Justice Oliver Wendell Holmes, Jr. set the stage for arbitrary handling of students when he ruled that public school interests superceded the rights of students. Principals had the legal right to admit or expel students at their whim. When school systems provided alternative education programs, they were usually segregated classrooms designated for problem students. In 1909, Elizabeth Farrell described the first New York City special education classroom:

The first class was made up of the odds and the ends of a large school. There were the over-age children, the so-called naughty children, and the dull, and the stupid children. They were taken from any and every school grade. The ages ranged from 8 to 16 years. They were the children who could not get along in school. They were typical of a large number of children who even today are forced directly or indirectly out of school; they were the children who were interested in street life; many of them earned a good deal of money in one way or another. While some of them had been in trouble with the police, as a class they could not be characterized as criminal. They had varied interests but the school, as they found it, had little or nothing for them. (p. 297)

Farrell's description of self-contained special education classes rings as true today as it did in the early twentieth century. Approximately 25% of special education students were placed in segregated special education programs that allowed for little or no interaction with non-disabled students (U.S. Department of Education, 2000).

THE INDIVIDUALS WITH DISABILITIES EDUCATION ACT

A combination of research and advocacy efforts on behalf of children with disabilities finally hit the mark in 1975. Following a flurry of class action suits filed across the country, Congress passed the Individuals with Disabilities Education Act (IDEA). This far-reaching legislation guaranteed all students, regardless of disability, the right to a free and appropriate education in the least restrictive environment. The quiet revolution had won its greatest victory, but as time went by, it became clear that there were more battles to be waged.

Today, the fact that students with disabilities have a right to attend public school is a foregone conclusion. Children and adults with disabilities are no longer relegated to the back wards of institutions, but their quest for normalcy continues. The separation of public school students into groups of "normal" and "abnormal" continues each year. In 2001, six million students were placed in special education programs. Many of these students have legitimate disabilities, but others do not. Many experts believe that a large number of public school students with reading problems are misidentified as learning disabled. The misplacement of students in special education is a serious problem. Misplacement dilutes resources and squanders money that is meant for disabled students. Some students are misplaced because special education is a convenient and out-of-the-way place for students with discipline problems. Others are misplaced because educational evaluations are unreliable. Still others are misplaced because special education teachers want to extend a helping hand to their regular education colleagues.

WHO ARE STUDENTS WITH DISABILITIES?

There are 13 categories of disabilities covered by the Individuals with Disabilities Education Act. Figure 2.1 lists each disability and percentage of placements in and outside of the regular classroom. The 13 categories can be divided into two groups: developmentally disabled and mildly disabled. Youngsters with developmental disabilities are usually identified at birth or soon after. These are children who will require lifetime assistance. Developmental disabilities include orthopedic impairments such as cerebral palsy and spina bifida. Autism, blindness, and deafness are other examples of developmental disabilities.

Students are eligible for special education beginning at age 3 and can continue in special education services up to age 22. In most cases, students with developmental disabilities are placed in early childhood programs because their disability manifests itself at an early age. The best of these early programs integrate students who are non-disabled and students with disabilities. The rationale for early childhood inclusion is that students who are non-disabled provide good models for students with special needs. Children with developmental disabilities account for approximately 16%

Figure 2.1
Percentage of Students Ages 6 –21 With Disabilities
Served in Different Educational Environments

Disabilities	All Students With Disabilities	1999–2000 School Year Served Outside the Regular Classroom			Public Separate Facility
		<21% of the Day	21–60% of the Day	>60% of the Day	
Specific learning disabilities	50.4	48.3	67.4	39.2	9.9
Speech or language impairments	19.2	35.5	4.6	5.0	2.5
Mental retardation	10.8	3.2	11.3	26.9	23.3
Emotional disturbance	8.2	4.5	6.8	13.3	32.9
Multiple disabilities	2.1	0.5	1.4	4.5	16.8
Hearing impairments	1.3	1.1	0.9	1.5	3.6
Orthopedic impairments	1.3	1.2	1.0	1.7	2.3
Other health impairments	4.5	4.2	5.2	3.8	2.1
Visual impairments	0.5	0.5	0.3	0.4	1.1
Autism	1.2	0.5	0.6	2.9	4.9
Deaf-blindness	0.02	0.01	0.01	0.05	0.2
Traumatic brain injury	0.2	0.2	0.2	0.4	0.3
Development delay	New category; data not yet compiled				

Source: U.S. Department of Education, Office of Special Education Programs, Data Analysis System (DANS).

of all special education students (U.S. Department of Education, 1999).

The remaining 84% of special education students are usually not identified as requiring special education until they enter school and begin to encounter academic or social problems. These are students with mild disabilities. Students with mild disabilities include those with learning disabilities (by far the largest group), those with behavioral or emotional problems, those with mild mental retardation, and those with speech and language impairments. Another mild learning problem—attention deficit hyperactivity disorder (ADHD)—is not included as a category of disability in IDEA. However, many students with this disorder are enrolled in special education programs under one or the other of the following categories: "behavior disordered," "learning disabled," or "other health impairment." The latter category refers to medical conditions that impede participation in school activities.

WHY INCLUSION?

The legal mandate for inclusion is based on the directive in IDEA that requires all students with disabilities to be educated in the least restrictive environment. According to the 1997 amendments to the Individuals with Disabilities Education Act, "each State must establish procedures to assure that, to the maximum extent appropriate, children with disabilities . . . are educated with children who are not disabled, and that special education, separate schooling, or other removal of children with disabilities from the regular educational environment occurs only when the nature or severity of the disability is such that education in regular classes with the use of supplementary aids and services cannot be achieved satisfactorily."

Only when it is clear that a student will receive a more appropriate education in another type of setting is placement outside the regular classroom justified. The decision to educate students in more restrictive settings should be given careful consideration, because segregation creates its own set of problems.

Students in separate, self-contained special education programs are especially vulnerable to feelings of isolation and rejection by peers (Wenz-Gross & Siperstein, 1998). The case of Mr. Reilly may be instructive here. Mr. Reilly taught in an alternative public school for students with behavior and emotional problems. On all accounts, his program was a success. Students were learning and parents were pleased. One November morning, 12-year-old David stormed into the classroom. He threw his books on his desk and said, "I quit this f—ing school! I'm tired of kids calling me 'retard.'" He continued, "Every morning I stand on the corner with my friends; they take the regular bus and I take the 'retard' bus." Derek and James said the same thing happened to them. Gabrielle agreed. The students' experience had a profound effect on Mr. Reilly. He realized by developing a "model" special education program he had inadvertently contributed to the stigmatization.

Determining how and where to educate students with disabilities presents a complicated decision. Each family and school system must find a way to balance the principle of appropriate education with the principle of least restrictive environment. The following chapter provides some basic guidelines for navigating the complicated legal and educational landscape of special education.

Chapter 3

Navigating the
Special Education Maze

Since 1975, when the Individuals with Disabilities Education Act (IDEA) was passed, special education has grown into a multi-billion-dollar enterprise. Presently, over 6,000,000 students aged 3 to 21 receive special education services, and the number grows each year (U.S. Department of Education, 2002). In order to be eligible for special education, a student must be certified as disabled according to criteria outlined by individual states. IDEA established definitions for specific disabilities, but states have the leeway to develop their own regulations and to determine how a disability is defined. The variations between IDEA and state criteria mean that a child can be declared disabled in one state, move to another state with different criteria, and be declared non-disabled. Moreover, even within specific states, a special education student can be de-certified as in need of special education because each school system is free to choose its own evaluation procedures, including type of tests and observational procedures.

This shifting of regulatory groundwork is confusing for both families and educators. However, three key legal principles form the basis of IDEA, and each, by law, must be included in every state's special education regulations. These principles anchor student and family rights in firm legal bedrock and help ensure that no major decision about the direction of a special education program can proceed without parental consent. The three stabilizing principles are as follows:

1. Free and Appropriate Education

2. Least Restrictive Environment

3. Due Process

FREE AND APPROPRIATE EDUCATION

The Individuals with Disabilities Education Act mandates a free and appropriate education for every student with a disability. No matter how severe the disability, no child can be denied an appropriate public school education. The form a student's education takes will be dictated by the nature of the disability and the educational decisions made by the school system and families. For a student with a developmental disability, such as severe cerebral palsy, an appropriate education might include a combination of services designed to teach the child to feed himself, communicate through sign language, and operate a customized computer. Meeting the needs of students with complex and lifelong disabilities requires the resources of a range of professionals including physical therapists, occupational therapists, and speech pathologists.

Meanwhile, students with mild disabilities, such as dyslexia, can manage with adaptive instruction. What is "appropriate" for each student is determined by the goals and services outlined in a student's individual education plan (IEP).

The Individual Education Plan

The IEP is the solution to the vexing problem—how do you provide an "appropriate" individualized education for six million students with disabilities? The key is parental consent. The parent decides if a special education intervention is appropriate. No student can be placed in a special education program or commence special education services without a caretaker signature on the IEP. Each IEP includes the following:

- A description of educational performance, including a statement about how the student's disability affects participation in the general regular education curriculum.

- A statement of annual goals accompanied by measurable and specific objectives for meeting those goals, including regular classroom participation.

- A description of additional services that will be made available to meet the student's special needs (for example, one-on-one aid, physical therapy, specialized equipment).

- A statement regarding the extent of general curriculum involvement and support services needed to meet annual goals and to participate in extracurricular activities.

- An explanation, if the student is not placed in a regular classroom, of the reason for alternative placement. If the student needs to be transported, the transportation method must also be detailed, and if the student has a behavior or emotional problem, a behavior management plan should be attached to the IEP.

It might seem that the IEP is a federally mandated "wish list," but it is not. A Supreme Court decision in 1982 put the brakes on the notion that free and appropriate education meant that parents of students with disabilities could ask for and receive whatever adaptations they felt were necessary.

The Rowley Decision. Amy Rowley received special education services due to a severe hearing impairment. She was enrolled full-time in first grade. She received special tutoring. Additionally, her school provided an amplification device to enhance her hearing. Amy could also read lips; however, Amy missed information every time her teacher turned away. Despite her difficulties, Amy was making passing grades.

Amy's parents, however, were not pleased with the quality of Amy's education. They filed a civil action in Federal District Court claiming that Amy was not receiving an appropriate education. The Court agreed with the parents. In the judgment, the Court said that an appropriate education includes an opportunity to achieve that is commensurate with opportunities provided to children without disabilities. The school system appealed the decision. The Federal Court of Appeals upheld this decision and the school district continued its appeal to the Supreme Court.

In 1982, the Supreme Court reversed the decisions of the lower courts (*Hendrick Hudson Dist. Bd. of Ed. v. Rowley*, 1982). In so doing, the Supreme Court upheld Congressional requirements for an IEP and stated that the IEP should reasonably be calculated to enable a child to achieve passing grades and be promoted. However, the Court said that the purpose of the federal special education law was to provide access to public education, but that the Act does not require a school system to *maximize* the potential of each disabled child (emphasis added). In so doing, the Court affirmed the due process rights of families. If parents did not agree with an IEP, they had the right to redress their grievances through certain procedural safeguards instituted by Congress. These procedural safeguards will be explained in the section on due process.

IEP Preparation

Every year, a student's IEP must be updated. This requires a meeting between families and school representatives. The amount of time that goes into preparing IEPs is extensive. A typical special education resource teacher might have a caseload of 30 students. That means 30 IEPs to write and 30 IEP meetings to attend. In April and May, when much of this activity occurs, teachers can spend as much time out of the classroom attending meetings as they do instructing students. This same involvement in IEP development can become a part of the inclusive regular-education teacher's responsibilities as well.

Before 1997, IDEA did not include a regular education teacher as a required member of an IEP decision team. Since the 1997 IDEA amendments, the IEP meeting for a student in an inclusive classroom must include one of a student's regular education teachers. Also, to the extent appropriate, the regular education teacher must participate in the development and revision of students' IEPs.

Specifically, the 1997 amendments to IDEA state:

- If a student has more than one regular education teacher, the school system may designate which teacher will attend IEP meetings.

- When elements of the IEP meeting include services not directly related to the inclusion classroom, the regular education teacher need not be required to participate in all decisions, be present throughout the entire meeting, or attend every meeting.

- The extent of the regular education teacher's participation in IEP meetings should be evaluated on a case-by-case basis.

- Each of a student's regular education teachers must be informed of his or her responsibilities related to implementing the IEP, including accommodations, modifications, and special supports required by the student.

Regardless of how much time the inclusive teacher spends in IEP development, he or she is still held accountable for student progress. Students cannot be failed if objectives are not met, nor can teachers be sued for students' unsatisfactory progress. But the IEP is still a legal contract and parents rightfully expect to see progress.

An average IEP is five to six pages long. Length is usually determined by the complexity of the disability. The IEP for a student with multiple disabilities can extend to 20 or more pages. In one instance, teachers in a residential school for students with emotional problems developed IEPs over a hundred pages long.

They went overboard because they were not clear on where the IEP left off and the school curriculum began. The purpose of the IEP is to spell out adaptations to the regular curriculum.

LEAST RESTRICTIVE ENVIRONMENT

When IDEA was passed in 1975, it was named the Education for All Handicapped Children Act. The fledgling law immediately caused a stir among teachers, who feared an influx of children with disabilities into their classrooms. The media heightened teacher anxiety by dubbing the new legislation "the mainstreaming law," implying that students with disabilities would be "mainstreamed" en masse into regular classrooms. The anticipated influx into regular education never materialized; rather, the number of students placed in special education programs climbed each year. By 2000, the special education population was more than double what it was in 1975 (U.S. Department of Education, 2002).

Neither the term "mainstreaming" nor the term "inclusion" appears in the Individuals with Disabilities Education Act. The term Congress used to refer to where students would be educated is the "least restrictive environment" (LRE). Least restrictive environment is a relative term. "Least restrictive" means students should be put in special education classrooms that are as close to normal as possible. For some students, the least restrictive environment might be part-time regular education classroom and part-time special education tutoring. For others, least restrictive might mean a self-contained special education classroom rather than residential placement. According to federal law, each school system has to offer a continuum of special education settings from least to most restrictive (see Figure 3.1). It is up to families and educators to decide which setting on the continuum is the best match for each student.

More restrictive settings include private schools (and residential programs) that cater to specific disabilities. A blind student in Massachusetts might attend Perkins School for the Blind; a deaf student might attend Clarke School for the Deaf. Public schools will send a student to a private program for two reasons: the school system does not provide the specialized service a student needs, or parents request the private placement because they feel the quality is better than what the public school has to offer.

Private education at the taxpayers' expense is big business. The typical private day school costs $30,000 and up per student per year, including transportation. Private residential programs cost $100,000 a year or more. Schools usually end up paying the tuition, and social services and family health insurance plans pick up the residential costs. The placement of a child in a private program costs a school system many thousands of dollars over the course of the student's education. With such vast amounts of money involved, it is easy to see why school administrators support inclusion. A successful inclusion program that supplants private placements can save a school district a lot of money.

When making a decision about special education placement, families and school systems must balance the legal requirements of an appropriate education with the legal requirements of least restrictive environment. If a regular classroom cannot provide an appropriate education, other options in the least restrictive continuum must be considered. One of the reasons so many special education advocates pushed for inclusion was that some special education programs had become "dead-end" classrooms where

Figure 3.1

Federally Mandated Special Education Settings

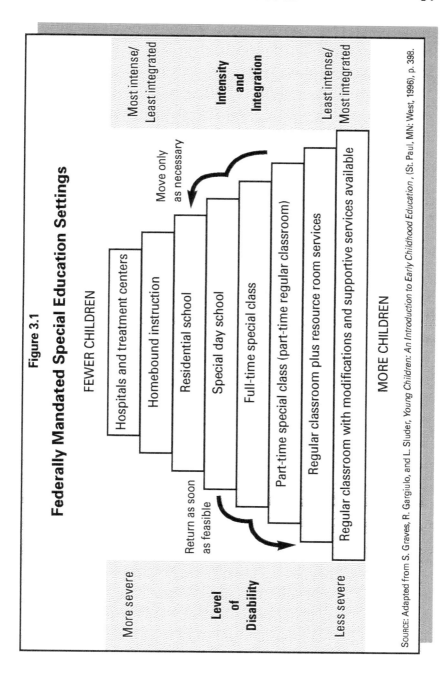

FEWER CHILDREN

Hospitals and treatment centers

Homebound instruction

Residential school

Special day school

Full-time special class

Part-time special class (part-time regular classroom)

Regular classroom plus resource room services

Regular classroom with modifications and supportive services available

MORE CHILDREN

Move only as necessary

Return as soon as feasible

Most intense/ Least integrated

Intensity and Integration

Least intense/ Most integrated

More severe

Level of Disability

Less severe

Source: Adapted from S. Graves, R. Gargiulo, and L. Sluder, *Young Children: An Introduction to Early Childhood Education,* (St. Paul, MN: West, 1996), p. 398.

students were placed and forgotten. Self-contained classrooms and alternative schools for students with behavioral and emotional problems have been singled out for their lack of quality services (Knitzer, Steinberg, & Fleisch, 1990). However, an inclusive classroom can also become a dead end, particularly if classroom resources and support are inadequate. The key issue is not where a student is placed, but the quality of education provided. If a student will not receive an appropriate education in a regular classroom, then inclusion is a bad idea and possibly illegal as well.

High-Stakes Tests

The political movement to increase school accountability by testing students and publicizing the results puts pressure on both special and regular educators to show positive results. In the past, school superintendents routinely excused special education students from state or locally required achievement tests. Now, due to political pressure by inclusion advocates, special education students throughout the country are required to participate in mandated testing right along with peers who are non-disabled. For a school system with a small special education population, mandated participation is manageable. But many school systems—especially those in urban settings—have high special education percentages, up to 15 or 20% (U.S. Department of Education, 2002).

Some states require students to pass standardized tests as a graduation requirement. Massachusetts, for instance, requires students with disabilities, just like their peers who are non-disabled, to pass the Massachusetts Comprehensive Assessment System (MCAS) as a graduation requirement. Results from 2001 show that of the 39,405 suburban and small town regular education students who took the MCAS, 94% met the passing cutoff score for English and 90% passed mathematics. Meanwhile 10,967 urban students passed at a rate of 71% in English and 62% in math. Of Massachusetts' 10,196 special education students, 47% passed English and 39% passed math (Hayward, 2002). Inclusive teachers face a stiff challenge as they attempt to adequately prepare their special education students for these high-stakes tests.

DUE PROCESS

One of the distinctive features of special education is the major role played by families. Caretaker consent is required for every significant decision, from initial referral for a special education evaluation to placement in a special education program. This parent power is unprecedented in American education and is one of the least understood aspects of IDEA. Parents do not always win disputes with school systems, but if they know their rights and act on them, they can be a force. Well-informed, committed parents can turn a school system on its head when they exercise all their legal options. Numerous disputes have landed in court with some working their way up the judicial ladder all the way to the Supreme Court. Among important parental due process rights are the following:

- The right to refer their child for special education services.

- The right to bring an advocate to all meetings.

- The right to participate in the design of their child's IEP.

- The right to refuse an IEP.

- The right to appeal all school system decisions through the State Department of Education and civil courts if necessary.

- The right to request an independent evaluation.

- The right to request a special education evaluation.

- The right to refuse a special education evaluation.

- The right to examine all of their child's school records.

- The right to have their child educated in the least restrictive environment.

- The right to expect full cooperation from the school system.

TERMINATION OF SPECIAL EDUCATION SERVICES

IDEA does not include specific language regarding graduation, but the 1997 amendments put greater emphasis on students' participating in the general curriculum and in state- and district-wide assessment of student achievement. IDEA regulations state:

- Because special education services can continue through age 21, graduation from high school is considered a change in placement and it requires parent/guardian written consent.

- A student's right to a free and appropriate education is terminated with a regular high school diploma.

- A student's right to a free and appropriate education is not terminated by any special graduation certificate or diploma.

- When students reach age 14, school systems are obligated to include transition plans in student IEPs. These transition plans spell out educational, vocational, and employment training needs.

- Students are required to participate in state-mandated assessments along with their peers who are non-disabled.

These listed rights under IDEA provide a framework for family, student, and school system cooperation. Changes in laws and regulations that affect educational services can be monitored through the Web site of the Office of Special Education and Rehabilitative Services: http://www.ed.gov/about/offices/list/osers/index.html.

The following section contains some frequently asked questions and answers that can help guide service providers and family members through the inclusion process.

INCLUSION: FREQUENTLY ASKED QUESTIONS

Q: *Why advocate for inclusion?*

A: Some consider inclusion an ethical choice. These advocates believe that separate education programs for disabled and non-disabled is an institutionalized form of segregation. Others support inclusion because they believe that a normal school experience is the best preparation for participation in mainstream society. Still others support inclusion because research studies (cited throughout this book) have documented the benefits of inclusion for disabled and non-disabled students alike. Finally, the Individuals with Disabilities Act (IDEA) requires that educators and families consider the regular classroom as the first special education placement option.

Q: *What is the difference between inclusion and mainstreaming?*

A: Inclusion means the student spends most of the day in the regular classroom. All special education services are delivered in the regular classroom. Mainstreaming means that the student spends a portion of the day in the regular classroom and receives special education services from a specialist outside the regular classroom.

Q: *Does inclusion work?*

A: Yes, if the proper supports are put in place. The most critical supports are administrative leadership, adequate planning time, in-service training, parental support, and effective collaboration between regular and special education personnel.

Q: *What are the arguments for inclusion?*

A: There are several arguments for inclusion. First, research on best teaching practices shows that students who receive their special education services in the regular classroom do better both academically and socially than students who are segregated in special education programs. Second, almost half of all students who receive special education services spend 80% of their day in the regular classroom anyway. These students receive "pull-out" special services and then return to the regular classroom. Third, students who are at risk for school failure and future special education placement benefit from the extra special education resources provided by an inclusion program (U.S. Department of Education, 2002).

Q: *What are the potential problems with inclusion?*

A: Teacher perception of students with disabilities is a key variable in determining success or failure. Seventy-one percent of regular education teachers do not feel qualified to teach in inclusion programs. Also, merging the requirements of a student's individual education plan (IEP) and the general curriculum is challenging (Marino, Miller, & Monahan, 1996). Students with disabilities have specific goals established in their IEPs that are not part of the general education curriculum. For example, there might be an emphasis on career education skills for older students and an emphasis on developmental goals for younger students.

Q: *What is the main reason why inclusion programs founder?*

A: Inclusion programs most often founder when teachers are assigned to inclusion programs by directive and without adequate administrative support.

Q: *Does the Individuals with Disabilities Education Act (IDEA) mandate inclusion for all students with disabilities?*

A: Placement decisions must balance the two principles of appropriate education and least restrictive environment. However, IDEA does state that an inclusive classroom should be the first option considered in determining the least restrictive environment, and if inclusion is not the selected placement, the school system must explain why.

Q: *Is inclusion a policy that schools can elect or not elect to adopt?*

A: No, inclusion is based on individual student need as outlined in the student's IEP.

Q: *Can a school use a lack of resources as a rationale for not providing a student with an inclusive program?*

A: Lack of adequate personnel or resources is not an acceptable reason for failure to provide inclusion, according to the U.S. Department of Education's policy guidelines. IDEA specifically states that a student can be denied an inclusive placement only if the severity of the disability is such that even with supplementary aids and services, the student would not receive an appropriate education.

Q: *Can a school system argue that a segregated program is qualitatively superior to an inclusive program?*

A: Placement decisions must be based on individual needs, not program attributes. The school system must demonstrate that the superior services cannot feasibly be provided in the inclusive classroom.

Q: *Should all students be included full time in the regular classroom?*

A: Not necessarily. The Individuals with Disabilities Education Act (IDEA) requires that full-time inclusion be the first option explored; however, the federal law also requires that every school system provide a continuum of special education placements from least restrictive (full-time regular classrooms) to most restrictive (residential placements).

Q: *What types of students are most often placed in separate programs?*

A: Students with behavior disorders and students with developmental problems are most frequently put in separate programs.

Q: *Is it common practice to place students in separate special education programs where they are segregated by disability?*

A: Overall, students with disabilities are placed in less restrictive environments, but placement decisions continue to be influenced by race, age, and disability. Elementary students, for example, are most likely to be included in regular classrooms. In 1999 to 2000, 76% of students with emotional/behavioral disabilities, 89% of students with multiple disabilities, and 86% of students with mental retardation spent most of their school days in separate special education programs (U.S. Department of Education, 2002).

Q: *Is inclusion more appropriate for students with mild disabilities such as a learning disability than for students with a developmental disability such as autism?*

A: In the 1983 case *Roncker v. Walter* the judge determined that placement decisions should be based on individual need, not type or degree of disability. School districts that place students in programs solely on the basis of disability violate federal law. It is not enough for a school system to claim a separate program is superior. The school system must also demonstrate that the "superior" services cannot be provided in the inclusive setting. This is called the *principle of portability*. The intent is to end the practice of automatic placement of students based on type of disability in separate special education programs.

Q: *How do a student's family and school determine if inclusion is the right placement?*

A: IDEA requires that two key principles be balanced: appropriate education and least restrictive environment. Full-time placement in the regular classroom is the least restrictive environment, but it might not meet the appropriate education standard.

Q: *Do families have to prove to schools that a child is capable of functioning within an inclusive setting?*

A: In *Oberti v. Board of Education of the Borough of Clementon School District*, a U.S. circuit court ruled that the school system had to prove why a student with Down syndrome could not be taught in an inclusive classroom; the family was not required to prove why he *could* be taught in this environment.

Q: *Do most parents want their children educated within inclusive classrooms?*

A: Sometimes parents request more restrictive placements. Alternative private schools for students with learning disabilities are one example of a more restrictive environment that parents sometimes request.

Q: *Does inclusion eliminate the need for special education teachers?*

A. Special educators continue to play an important role, usually as co-teachers and consultants. The focus of the special educator turns from remediation to collaboration.

Q: *What does collaboration mean?*

A: Typically the special educator co-teaches with regular educators or functions as a consultant.

Q: *What factors help collaboration work?*

A: Key factors are a willingness to work together and enthusiasm.

Q: *What role do non-special education peers play in an inclusion program?*

A: Peers are vital inclusion resources. Research on peer tutoring, for example, reports consistent improvement in academics for tutor and tutee alike.

Q: *Do students with disabilities need to keep up with regular education students in an inclusive classroom?*

A: Students do not need to meet any specific prerequisites for inclusion. For example, a student who cannot speak because of cerebral palsy could participate in a history class through the use of augmentative communication devices. Participation can be adapted for individual students with supplemental aids and services.

Q: *Does the inclusion success rate vary with disability?*

A: Students with physical disabilities, health impairments, and learning disabilities are those identified most often as succeeding in inclusion programs. Students with mental retardation and those with behavioral/emotional disorders have had less success. But success rates vary more with quality of programs than type of disability.

Q: *Why are there more difficulties involved with including students with behavioral/emotional disorders and mental retardation?*

A: Students with behavioral/emotional disabilities present discipline problems that many regular education teachers are ill equipped or not ready to deal with. Why students with mental retardation do not have a successful inclusion rate may have to do with stereotypes and low expectations for success.

Q: *Are students with severe developmental disabilities the most difficult to include in regular classrooms?*

A: No, teachers have the most difficulty including students with behavior disorders, especially those who have previously been placed in self-contained special education programs. These students require sophisticated classroom management skills.

Q: *Are students with behavior disorders best served in self-contained special education classrooms?*

A: No, the best option is to avoid removing these youngsters from the regular classroom in the first place. Most segregated programs for students with behavior disorders are an educational dead end—with a 50% dropout rate (U.S. Department of Education, 2001). Prevention rather than remediation is the solution.

Individual Education Plans (IEPs)

Q: *What is an IEP?*

A: An IEP is an individual education plan. No student can be placed in a special education program without an IEP signed by a parent or guardian.

Q: *What are the contents of an IEP?*

A: An IEP contains a statement about the student's learning style; a list of annual goals and objectives; a description of supplemental supports, aids, and services; mention of special accommodations; and an indication of the special education placement.

Q: *What does the phrase "supplemental supports, aids, and services" mean?*

A: "Supports, aids, and services" refers to a variety of methods and materials that schools are required to provide to assist in the instruction of students. They include, but are not limited to, paraprofessionals, assistive technology, counseling, adapted materials, speech, and occupational and physical therapy.

Q: *How is "appropriate education" determined?*

A: The IEP spells out how and where special education services will be delivered. By signing the IEP, a parent or guardian is agreeing that the IEP is appropriate.

Q: *Who determines a student's IEP?*

A: A student's parent or guardian meets with school personnel to design the IEP.

Q: *Do regular education teachers attend IEP meetings?*

A: If a regular education teacher is helping to provide special services, that teacher should attend and participate. If more than one regular education teacher is involved, the principal can appoint a representative.

Q: *How can professionals deal effectively with parents at IEP meetings?*

A: Parents need information presented with a minimum of educational and psychological jargon. Parents report feeling intimidated at IEP meetings. Professionals can facilitate parental involvement by being positive and constructive, rather than spending time telling parents everything that is wrong with their child.

Q: *Can students participate in their IEP meeting?*

A: At the age of 14, students have the legal right to participate in their IEP meetings.

Discipline

Q: *What are the legal requirements for dealing with a disruptive student with special needs?*

A: A student with special needs can be suspended for 10 or fewer days for disciplinary reasons and 45 or fewer days for drugs or weapons infractions. If suspensions are recurrent and go beyond 10 or 45 days respectively, the school system must do an assessment of the student's behavioral needs and implement a behavior intervention plan. If the behavior is a manifestation of the student's disability, the IEP must be redesigned (including a possible change in placement); if the behavior problem is found not to be a manifestation of a disability, the student can be disciplined in the same way as students who are non-disabled.

Q: *Can a student with a disability be expelled from school?*

A: If a student brings a weapon or drugs to school, he or she can be unilaterally placed in an alternative setting for 45 days by a school administrator. This allows time for an IEP team to review the offense and determine an appropriate placement. The alternative setting needs to provide educational services. If the student infraction has nothing to do with the student's disability, he or she can be treated the same as a regular education student.

Q: *What if a student on an IEP brings a weapon to school and immediate action is needed?*

A: The student can be placed unilaterally by school administration in an alternative education placement for up to 45 days. Placement may also be determined by a hearing officer.

Other Issues

Q: *Are inclusion programs more expensive than separate special education programs?*

A: In the short term, inclusion can be more expensive, especially when the inclusion classroom is set up with a special education teacher and regular education teacher co-teaching all day in the same classroom. Over the long term, this co-teaching model provides preventive intervention for students at risk for special education referral, evaluation, and placement. (One special education evaluation can cost a school system $500.) Decreasing special education referrals will, in the long run, save a lot of money. Money-saving results include lowering special education transportation costs, the merging of special and regular education budgets, a more unified administrative system, fewer placements in expensive private programs, and less need to rent and construct additional classrooms for separate special education programs.

As the above questions and answers indicate, inclusion is a multifaceted issue. The next chapter describes key issues to address in order to establish a successful inclusion program.

Chapter 4

Qualities of Successful
Inclusion Programs

INCLUSION REPRESENTS THE DEMOCRATIC IDEALS of equality and diversity. Within successful inclusion programs, students learn to value differences in appearance, behavior, and ability. There is a widely held suspicion that inclusion will cause students without disabilities to lose ground academically. To the contrary, the research on successful inclusion programs indicates that there is no decline in academic performance of students who are non-disabled. In well-organized inclusion programs, students with disabilities make significant social and academic gains (Baker, Wang, & Walberg, 1994; Brinker, 1983; Gartner & Lipsky, 1999; McGregor & Vogelsberg, 1998; Stainback & Stainback, 1990).

The National Longitudinal Transition Study of Special Education Students (NLTS) tracked the post-school progress of 8,000 young people with physical disabilities. Students who had been included full time in regular education were 43% more likely to be competitively employed after graduation than peers who had spent only half their time in regular education. The included students were also 41% more likely to be fully participating members of their communities than were students who attended separate special education programs (Wagner, Blackorby, Cameto, & Newman, 1993).

Anecdotal benefits of inclusion abound. The following is a brief sampling of the myriad ways that inclusion can enhance the quality of school for learners with and without disabilities:

- Third graders in Atlanta, Georgia, learned to sign along with a student with autism.

- High school students with developmental disabilities in West Springfield, Massachusetts, ran a coffee shop that was the hub of social life in the school.

- Teachers in a San Diego sixth grade classroom used co-operative learning activities to help a student with multiple disabilities form friendships with his non-disabled peers.

- A survey of more than 1,000 middle and high schools students indicated that 38% had friends with severe disabilities (Hendrickson, Shokoshi-Yekta, Hamre-Nietupsk; In Gable, 1996)

- Teachers in Missoula, Montana, used folk tales to teach social studies in an inclusive third grade that integrated students with ADD, learning disabilities, and behavior disorders (Wasta, Scott, Marchand-Martella, & Harris, 1999).

- Students at Edward Smith, an inclusive elementary school in Syracuse, New York, scored in the ninetieth percentile in state mandated achievement tests.

Inclusion is an educational melding of resources, ideas, and aspirations. An inclusive community strives to honor diversity and accepts differences as a part of the natural order of things. True to the democratic process, successful inclusion programs require the talents of the entire educational community—administrators, teachers, support staff, students, and parents. Successful inclusion programs are characterized by strong administrative leadership and a sense of community that lead to a commitment to academic excellence.

ADMINISTRATIVE LEADERSHIP

Inclusive classrooms require modification of preconceived notions about how students learn and how instruction is organized. In their article "Teaching students to be part of a democratic society" (1994), Calabrese and Barton write, "What we need now are people committed to each other in solidarity—people bound to each other who are willing to experience the bumpy road of diversity, the pain of debate, and the struggle to learn to live together in a society open to differences" (p. 55). Such fundamental change requires dynamic leadership.

The building administrator, more than any other single individual, must be committed to inclusion efforts. In an interview published in the Harvard Education Letter (1996), Tom Hehir, director of the federal Office of Special Education makes that clear. "We have found," he explains, "that one of the main factors in successful inclusion is the support of the principal and the administration" (p. 14). Administrative commitment to inclusion needs to be demonstrated in both words and deeds.

Creating a Vision

Leadership begins with a vision of what inclusion can mean to a school. The principal's philosophy frames issues and determines how decisions will be made. The fundamental political issue the principal faces is whether to dictate change or share decision-making. As every administrator knows, sharing control is tricky and can lead to unintended consequences. The principal needs to make a realistic appraisal of staff to determine which decisions will be shared and which decisions will be unilateral.

The advantage of joint planning is increased commitment on the part of teachers. It is unlikely that teachers will embrace organizational change on the magnitude needed for a successful inclusion program without participating in some planning decisions. Teachers' three most common complaints about inclusion are that they are coerced into an inclusive model, that they are not supported by the administration, and that not enough time is scheduled for planning. While inclusion by fiat gets things up and running quickly, resentments will undermine program effectiveness. Likewise, a lukewarm administrative attitude towards inclusion diminishes teacher enthusiasm. Without strong administrative support, staff morale erodes and inclusion efforts wither.

Because leadership issues are multi-layered and complex, the best strategy is to start small. A pilot program provides opportunities to identify resources, iron out wrinkles, and evaluate results. Visiting other inclusion programs with prospective inclusion teachers is an excellent way to begin planning. Nothing beats seeing an abstract idea in operation to allay anxieties and inspire new ideas. Some of the key questions that need to be dealt with during the planning stages are:

- What are teachers' in-service needs?

- How will classroom routines be changed?

- When will involved staff have time to plan and consult?

- What special steps are needed to prepare students?

- How will the inclusion program be described to parents?

- How will paraprofessionals be used effectively?

. . . and perhaps most important:

- Who will teach in the inclusion program?

- How will teachers plan together?

There is no rubric for these questions. The best solutions are ones worked out together by the participants—administration, teachers, and support staff. Embracing different perspectives helps establish a sense of collaboration that is critical for success.

Selecting Inclusion Teachers

Inclusion requires participation by all significant parties— students and adults alike. For many teachers, collaboration with peers is a novel experience. Teachers can spend an entire career doing their best work without the company of fellow professionals. Like nobles in medieval feudal states, teachers tend to their duties in adjacent territories divided by thick walls of cement. Making the transition from solitary teaching to collaborative teaching is a major adjustment.

Regular and special educators need to communicate about a host of details including IEP objectives, teaching methods, routines for integrating students within learning activities, and behavior management procedures. Additionally, there is input from a raft of support professionals whose services are mandated by students' IEPs. For teachers who are accustomed to running their own classrooms free from outside intrusion, collaboration means significant change. At the most fundamental level is the issue of control. Teachers who are not ready to change their orientation from solitary to collaborative teaching are unlikely candidates for inclusion programs. In the epilogue to his poem "The Age of Anxiety," W. H. Auden (1947) wrote about the difficulties of personal change:

> *We would rather be ruined than changed*
> *We would rather die in our dread*
> *Than climb the cross of the moment*
> *And let our illusions die.* (p. 17)

Inclusion requires teachers to do things differently. Not everyone is cut out to be an inclusion teacher. Forcing a teacher who is accustomed to working alone to collaborate with others is an unlikely formula for a successful inclusion program. The most negative feelings expressed about inclusion come from teachers who were forced into their role. Selecting teachers who share the inclusion philosophy and who are willing to make a commitment to collaboration is the most critical decision an administrator can make.

Qualities that characterize a good teacher candidate for inclusion programs include:

- an accepting attitude towards students with disabilities

- high expectations for all students

- ability to work with students at different ability levels

- desire to work collaboratively with other professionals

- knowledge of disabling conditions and special education procedures

- effective classroom management skills
- ability to implement activity-based learning experiences

Special Education-General Education Collaboration

Inclusion requires a reworking of the traditional responsibilities of general and special educators. Just as inclusion integrates students with and without disabilities, inclusion also binds teachers together. Three basic models of general and special education are co-teaching, consultation, and teaming.

Co-Teaching. Within the co-teaching model, the special and general education teachers share classroom responsibilities. Rather than dividing students into groups of those with disabilities and those without, the co-teachers organize activities to integrate students within each lesson. Often co-teachers divide responsibilities according to their academic interests. For example, the special educator might plan reading and language arts lessons while the general educator organizes math, science, and social studies lessons. When it comes to implementation, each assists the other.

Other examples of co-teaching include whole group (one teaches, the other monitors), shared presentations, teacher-directed centers, remedial/enrichment teaching, and parallel teaching.

Students can be grouped in a variety of ways including 1) one group with a lead and floating teacher, 2) two groups with each teacher covering the same content, 3) two groups (one teacher reviewing material the other teaching alternative information), and 4) multiple groups with both teachers monitoring.

Key concerns to be addressed are the grading system, classroom rules, allocation of space, ways of communicating with parents, and scheduling time to co-plan. Because two full-time teachers are located in one classroom, the co-teaching model is more costly than consultation. The additional expense can be mitigated by increasing the total number of students and including students with disabilities who previously were placed in expensive alternative special education programs.

Co-teaching can be the most or least satisfying arrangement, depending on how well the two teachers cooperate. The matching of teachers with good communication skills is crucial. For most teachers, this will be the first time they have shared duties with another professional. Many issues will surface, especially during the first year, which will need to be worked through. When co-teachers do not get along, interpersonal problems threaten the success of the entire program.

The following recommendations can help maintain a smooth working relationship between co-teachers:

- Learn each other's interests and areas of expertise.

- Develop a plan for sharing instructional responsibilities.

- Establish a regular meeting time and stick with it.

- Determine how different instructional approaches can be used during the day.

- Establish clear-cut learning goals and objectives.

- Determine how to organize classroom space to encourage general and special education students to work together.

- Explore ways of integrating curriculum areas through multi-disciplinary courses and thematic units.

- Develop a procedure for promptly dealing with professional differences.

Consultation. Instead of working directly with students, the consulting teacher meets with several inclusion teachers on a regularly scheduled basis. This approach is best in small schools with low numbers of special education students and a generally small student population. The consultant must have demonstrated expertise in adapting classroom instruction and in classroom management. Moreover, the consultant needs excellent communication skills and the ability to tend to issues immediately. To the financially strapped administrator, the consultation model is appealing. Two key issues will determine the success of the consultant approach: how teachers feel about consultant recommendations, and the reliability of conference schedules.

There is a potential imbalance of power when professionals assist other professionals. Sometimes the helper is perceived as the "expert" and the person who is helped is perceived as lacking in some way. When a person voluntarily asks for advice, the imbalance is less problematic, but unsolicited advice can lead to resentment. Imagine a 23-year-old special education teacher fresh out of college consulting a group of veteran teachers, and you will get the picture. It is vital that the consultant not be viewed as the "expert" and the inclusion teacher as correspondingly less capable. Consultants and classroom teachers are partners. Titling the consultant "collaboration teacher" is one way of avoiding the implication that the consultant is more knowledgeable than the classroom teacher.

The consulting teacher should expect to

- conduct regularly scheduled meetings with inclusion teachers.

- model lessons in the inclusion classroom.

- assist with locating supplies and materials.

- conduct parent training.

- provide technology assistance.

- identify issues for administrative attention.

- substitute to allow classroom teachers to attend meetings.

Teaming. This method is often used in secondary schools. The special education teacher is assigned to a team of teachers. The team meets on a regular basis. Special education input can be offered by a consultant or co-teacher, depending on content material and priorities. It is vital that on a regular basis the special education teacher work directly with students who are non-disabled. This will alleviate the tendency to "pigeonhole" the special education teacher as a teacher of only students with disabilities.

The special education teacher in a team should expect to

- provide students with information about how a disability affects performance.

- spell out IEP goals and objectives and explain how the IEP relates to the general curriculum.

- recommend instructional accommodations and model new strategies.

- coordinate delivery of special education services such as counseling, speech therapy, and occupational therapy.

- suggest grading and test-taking changes.

- provide support with managing student behavior.

- stay active in team member classrooms.

Support Services. Regardless of the collaborative model selected, specialist support staff play an important role as well. These staff members include reading teachers, speech and language specialists, occupational therapists, physical therapists, counselors, and paraprofessionals. Coordinating the efforts of support specialists takes attention to detail, clear communication, and adequate scheduling. For a classroom teacher who is accustomed to teaching alone, the presence of other adults in the classroom presents a change of working conditions. Thus, inclusion teachers find themselves adding another new title to their job descriptions: supervisor. Inclusion programs with students who have physical disabilities or multiple disabilities in particular need adequate planning time to determine how several professionals can best work together. Once support professionals are scheduled for an inclusive classroom, they are responsible for fulfilling their part of the students' individual education plans. By arranging these services in small groups that include non-disabled students as well, support professionals can make significant contributions to the education of all students in the classroom.

To summarize, professionals' ability to collaborate plays a pivotal role in determining the success of an inclusion program. Attention to teacher attitude, emphasis on fostering collaborative relationships, and appropriate in-service training are priority inclusion concerns (Beattie, Anderson, & Antonak, 1997; Bennet & Deluca, 1997; Hammeken, 2000; Johnson & Pugach, 1995; Lanier & Lanier, 1996; Ritter, 1989). While the administrator leads an inclusive school, success or failure ultimately rests on the efforts of the entire school community. The "Inclusion Plan Checklist" (Figure 4.1) can help identify key inclusion criteria that should be assessed.

THE COMMUNITY CLASSROOM

Successful inclusion programs are sustained by a pervasive sense of community. An inclusive community is one in which all students feel accepted and are encouraged to care for each other. Teachers promote community by allowing students to participate more fully in classroom decisions than they typically can in traditional, teacher-controlled classrooms. Such leading questions as how should we decorate the room, what field trips should we take, and how can we get along together, encourage student input and help boost class morale. Within the classroom community, the emotional needs of the child are as important as the academic needs of the student. Basic needs such as trust and security that form a foundation for successful learning are nurtured in the community classroom.

The purpose of inclusion is to embrace different learners and convince them that they are part of a community of learners. Brendtro, Brokenleg, and Van Bockern (2001) identify four values of community inspired by Native American cultural values: belonging, mastery, independence, and generosity. These four values establish a communal basis for inclusion programs. They provide a moral compass to guide overall program development as well as day-to-day implementation. Belonging promotes acceptance. Mastery establishes high expectations for success. Independence sustains feelings of self-determination, and generosity fosters caring for others (see Figure 4.2).

Figure 4.1

Inclusion Plan Checklist

Rate each of the following inclusion criteria:

Administrative Checklist

<u>Criteria</u>	<u>Weak</u>	<u>Adequate</u>	<u>Good</u>	<u>Strong</u>
Appropriate setting	1	2	3	4
Admin. commitment	1	2	3	4
In-service training	1	2	3	4
Teacher commitment	1	2	3	4
Planning/meeting time	1	2	3	4
Classroom support	1	2	3	4
Compatibility	1	2	3	4
Student preparation	1	2	3	4
Family communication	1	2	3	4
IEP development	1	2	3	4
Prof. communication	1	2	3	4
Formative evaluation	1	2	3	4
Recognition	1	2	3	4

Classroom Checklist

Clear IEP objectives	1	2	3	4
Behavior supports	1	2	3	4
Social skill objectives	1	2	3	4
Fostering of community	1	2	3	4
Meetings	1	2	3	4
Cooperative learning	1	2	3	4
Peer tutoring	1	2	3	4
Service	1	2	3	4
Shared decision-making	1	2	3	4
Other _____	1	2	3	4
Adult communication	1	2	3	4
Classroom resources	1	2	3	4
Technology	1	2	3	4
Adult decision-making	1	2	3	4
Support diversity	1	2	3	4

The goal of a classroom community is to promote the emotional development of children and inject a sense of purpose into the curriculum. Many students with disabilities feel estranged from peers and diminished by school failure. Special educators use the term "learned helplessness" to describe how school failure can undermine confidence in oneself as a competent individual. In order to reach their potential, students with special needs must be made to feel that they have a legitimate place among their peers and within the culture of the school.

Some traits that typify community in classrooms include:

- strong relationships between teacher and students.

- routines and procedures that allow students to participate in classroom decisions.

- a shared ethos of caring, concern, and support.

- emphasis on cooperative activities.

- an appreciation for cultural diversity.

The E, B, C of Community: Empowerment, Belonging, Cooperation

A community is a group of individuals who share a common interest and who rely on each other for mutual support. Solidarity among students is reinforced by classroom practices that give them opportunities to express their feelings and to make choices. Three principles that guide the development of classroom communities are empowerment, belonging, and cooperation.

Empowerment. Empowerment means allowing students to make some decisions about how they spend their day. Student

Figure 4.2
Circle of Courage

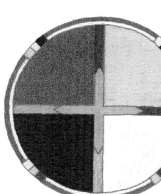

GENEROSITY

BELONGING

INDEPENDENCE

MASTERY

The Circle of Courage is a trademark of Circle of Courage, Inc.
Contact www.reclaiming.com or e-mail courage@reclaiming.com for more information.

empowerment increases motivation to learn, promotes student responsibility, and enhances student morale (Mendler, 2000). Consider the quality of student participation in extra-curricular activities. Students work on school newspapers, participate in debate clubs, and rehearse school plays because these activities are empowering. Providing students with choices and allowing them to pursue personal interests can transfer some of the spontaneous enthusiasm found in extra-curricular activities into the classroom. Teachers empower by

- allowing students to establish rules of conduct.

- permitting students to decorate areas of the classroom.

- asking for student input about how and when specific aspects of the curriculum will be taught.

- having regular discussions about classroom issues.

- giving students specific classroom maintenance and organizational responsibilities.

Belonging. Maslow (1970) believed that many of society's social problems could be traced to the failure to meet the basic human need of belonging. Glasser said, "Hungry students look for food, lonely students look for friends" (cited in Beck & Malley, 1998, p. 13). The Phi Delta Kappa Commission on Discipline (1982) found that vandalism, school drop-out, and chronic discipline problems were directly attributable to students feeling estranged from their school experience. John Steinbeck (1952) said, "The greatest terror a child can have is that he is not loved, and rejection is the hell he fears" (p. 18). Feelings of isolation put youngsters at risk as they progress through adolescence. If frustrated in healthy attempts to belong, young people will persevere in their attempts to connect with peers through drugs, alcohol, cults, and gangs.

Inclusion offers students the opportunity to forge friendships that will sustain them through difficult times. Successful inclusion requires close attention to how students relate to each other. The following recommendations are a good starting point for helping special education students feel they are a part of the group:

- Continually promote the idea that the class is a community.

- Change seat and small-group arrangements to sidetrack cliques and integrate students who are isolated.

- Recognize the contributions of every student to the classroom community on a regular basis.

- Minimize reward systems that are beyond the reach of special education students.

- Celebrate cultural diversity.

- Frankly explain aspects of disabling conditions.

- Discuss movies and videos that include various disabling conditions.

- Invite adults with disabilities to come to class to talk about their lives.

- Structure instructional and non-instructional interactions among all students.

- Share books and newspaper stories about people with disabilities.

- Recognize contributions to art and science by individuals with disabilities.

- Praise effort as much as achievement.

- Equally distribute teaching time among all students.

- Maintain high expectations.

- Remember that a disability is an impediment, not an excuse.

Conscious attention to integration of students for instruction is preferable to isolating students for special education tutoring within the regular classroom. Special education students would rather be placed in a separate special education program than endure the embarrassment of isolated special instruction in the regular classroom (Klinger, Vaughn, Schumm, Cohen, & Forgen, 1998). Some common mistakes made in non-inclusive classrooms are:

- separating students from their peers for special instruction.

- seating a paraprofessional next to a special education student for long periods during the day.

- seating special education students apart from peers.

- treating students with disabilities as if they were fragile.

Cooperation. Cooperation is the bridge that connects the individual need for empowerment with the social need for belonging. Cooperation, not competition, has propelled human civilization forward. Eons ago, cooperation in hunting, gathering, and safety was based on mutual need and survival. Cooperative farming spurred the building of villages and the formation of stable social communities. As a species, we prefer communal living to isolation. As our technologically linked world grows closer together, cooperation continues to be a unifying factor in advancing human culture.

Classrooms are a microcosm of society. In order to be productive, students need to be able to work together, to share resources, and to follow rules for getting along, just as citizens do in larger communities. Cooperation builds social competence. A socially competent individual is distinguished by the ability to develop interpersonal relationships and to work collaboratively with others. Gillies and Ashman (2000) have reported that "When students worked in cooperative groups, they were consistently more cooperative and helpful, used language that was more inclusive, and gave more explanations to assist understanding" (p. 748). Conversely, lack of social competence leads to a variety of behavior difficulties, such as chronic discipline problems, behavioral disorders, and delinquency (Rutherford, Quinn, & Mathur, 1998).

Teachers promote cooperation in the classroom by

- employing student-centered instructional methods such as brainstorming, meetings, cooperative learning, and peer tutoring.

- analyzing class group dynamics to determine the best way to organize learning groups.

- soliciting student feedback and suggestions for improving the classroom climate.

- modeling cooperative social skills through their interactions with other adults.

- highlighting cooperation rather than competition in class activities both in and outside the classroom.

- emphasizing group rather than individual goals.

A MODEL INCLUSION SCHOOL

Kensington Avenue Elementary School is located in a working class neighborhood about one-half mile from downtown Springfield, Massachusetts. Kensington has a 92% poverty rate and a 22% special needs rate. In 1999, Kensington was recognized by the Massachusetts governor as one of five most improved schools in the state. Throughout this 384-student K-5 school, students with special needs spend their entire day in regular classrooms. The principal, Tim Babcock, and staff are dedicated to the ideal that all students can learn together. A banner over the main doorway summarizes the spirit of Kensington: "Some goals are so worthy it is glorious to fail."

While other public schools in this western Massachusetts city have struggled with the statewide assessment tests (MCAS), Kensington students have excelled. In the 2000 administration of the MCAS, 26% of Springfield public school fourth grade students were proficient in English/Language Arts, and 12% were proficient in mathematics. At Kensington, 48% of fourth graders tested in the proficient range in English/Language Arts and 37% were proficient in mathematics.

Within each Kensington classroom, a regular education teacher and special education teacher work side by side. This co-teaching allows teachers to capitalize on their individual strengths and to experiment with new ideas. Instead of pulling students out for special education tutoring in the "dummy dungeon," as former students described the resource room, the school sends special education services to the students. All students, regular and special education alike, benefit from the influx of materials and personnel.

A typical day begins with a class meeting. Then students move on to work stations, where they work on prescribed learning activities or engage in small instructional groups. During the course of the school day, various professionals enter classrooms to work with students. The adjustment counselor, the speech and language teacher, the Title I teacher, and the physical therapist circulate among classrooms. No distinction is made between regular and special education students. All students benefit from the expertise each professional brings to the classroom.

The needs of special education students are addressed in small groups with regular education students. There is no homogeneous tracking at Kensington. Instructional groupings are fluid and based on the changing needs of students. Most important, teachers enjoy working together. Positive test scores at Kensington have provided objective validation for their efforts, but it is the quality of their daily experience that sets Kensington apart in the minds of teachers and staff. As one teacher remarked, "My co-teacher and I are co-dependent; it's so nice to work each day alongside someone you get along with." It is the sense of community, the belief that together they are doing good work, that more than any other attribute is the hallmark of success at Kensington Avenue Elementary.

The Responsive Classroom. Many successful inclusion programs utilize a specific educational model to organize routines and guide instruction. Kensington Elementary School uses the "Responsive Classroom" model (Elliot, 1993). The Responsive Classroom provides practical strategies for teaching students with diverse social and learning abilities. With its emphasis on developing a community within the classroom and its social skills curriculum, the Responsive Classroom is particularly well suited to a school with a diverse student body.

The Responsive Classroom approach highlights the following teaching element (The Responsive Classroom, n.d.):

- Morning Meeting: A daily routine that builds community, creates a positive climate for learning, and reinforces academic skills.

- Rules and Logical Consequences: A clear and consistent approach to discipline that fosters responsibility and self-control.

- Guided Discovery: A format for introducing materials that encourages inquiry, heightens interest, and teaches care of the school environment.

- Academic Choice: An approach to giving students choices in their learning that helps them become invested, self-motivated learners.

- Classroom Organization: Strategies for arranging materials, furniture, and displays to encourage independence, promote caring, and maximize student movement.

- Family Communication Strategies: Ideas for involving families as partners in their children's education.

Successful programs like the one at Kensington Avenue Elementary School demonstrate that inclusion programs offer more than an alternative way of providing special education services. Elizabeth Zylstra (2001), a second grade teacher in Idaho, was reluctant to include Bobby, a student with autism, in her classroom. During the year, she saw her class go through a transformation as she and her students who were non-disabled helped Bobby learn. As Bobby grew, so did his classmates and his teacher. Mrs. Zylstra described how the experience changed her perception of what "disability" means:

Bobby had his own personality and his own sense of humor. We laughed together, we became frustrated together, we helped one another learn, and we grew into a real community. As the year unfolded, the other students and I no longer saw Bobby as the boy who had autism, but as Bobby, a 2nd grader who had wishes, dreams, likes, and dislikes just like everyone else. (p. 75)

When administration, teachers, and students commit to working together, inclusive education enhances the learning experience for everyone. Most of all, inclusion demonstrates that a disability does not define a child; rather, inclusion provides young people with the opportunity to define themselves.

Chapter 5

Inclusive Teaching

LIKE PROSPECTORS SEARCHING FOR PRECIOUS STONES, educators are always searching for the best way to teach. And educators strive like prospectors to discriminate between fool's gold and the real thing. Many claims are staked about the best way to teach—whole language, phonics, direct instruction, constructivism, cooperative learning, computer-assisted instruction, learning styles, drill and repetition, multi-sensory instruction . . . the list goes on and on. Yet, for every teacher who strikes gold with a particular method, there is another one who goes bust.

Several years ago, I attended a meeting of special education college faculty and public school special education administrators. The administrators had some very specific complaints about new teachers. An administrator of a large urban school system was particularly unhappy with pre-service training. He said, "Every year I have to train our new teachers in the Orton-Gillingham method. We use Orton-Gillingham to teach our students with learning disabilities, and I'm tired of doing the colleges' job." Many of my higher education colleagues exchanged bemused glances. One instructional approach for that city's 3,700 students with learning disabilities seemed more like fool's gold than a shining example of individualized instruction.

Whenever someone asks me what is the best way to teach special education students, I think of the special education administrator who believed so fervently in the Orton-Gillingham approach. The Orton-Gillingham method was developed by a neurosurgeon to teach students with dyslexia. It is based on the premise that phonics is best taught through a combination of multi-sensory (visual, auditory, tactile, and kinesthetic) methods and systematic teacher instruction—a pretty good approach for some students; however, not all students with learning disabilities have dyslexia, nor do all students with learning disabilities succeed with the Orton-Gillingham method.

With all the claims and counterclaims about the best way to teach, how can a teacher decide what instructional approach is best? The research on this question is clear: Effective teaching methods are judged by the level of student participation (Brophy & Good, 1986). Simply put, students who are actively engaged in their learning succeed; those who are not, struggle. Engaged learning refers to explicit student behavior that indicates that students are thinking. Creative writing, brainstorming, contrasting ideas, creating projects, interacting with other students, and participating in teacher-student dialogue are examples of engaged learning. Although silent reading, oral reading, looking up answers to textbook questions, listening to teacher lectures, independent seat work, copying notes, and doing worksheets are commonplace activities, these are not necessarily engaged behaviors because they require little thought. Figure 5.1 shows methods of inclusive instruction that are more and less effective.

Figure 5.1

Methods for Inclusive Instruction

<u>More Effective</u>	<u>Less Effective</u>
Peer tutoring	Independent seat work
Active teaching and supervising	Lecturing, silent reading, answering textbook questions
Concrete activities	Worksheets
Cooperative learning groups	Independent group projects
Functional practice	Drill and repetition
Teaching learning strategies	Giving directions and assuming response
Outcome-based teaching	Modality teaching
Computer-assisted instruction	Educational games
Thematic lessons	Isolated subjects
Social skill instruction	Rewards and punishment

Derived from numerous sources including Murphy (2003), Hammeken (2000), and Marzano (2003).

Although the major part of each school day is allocated for instruction, the amount of time students actually spend engaged in learning is considerably less. Estimates of engaged learning time range from 45% to as little as 16% of the school day (Greenwood, 1991). Middle school students, for example, spend 75% of their classroom time and 90% of their homework time sitting and reading textbooks (Wenz-Gross & Siperstain, 1998). Such lengthy periods of passivity stifle engaged learning. Maria Montesorri, the famed Italian physician and educator, once said that the least useful educational tool is the chair. Sitting compresses the spinal cord, slows respiration, and induces fatigue.

Good teaching will trump learning problems every time. *No child is so severely disabled that he or she cannot learn one more thing.* The following principles of instruction embrace teaching methods that have proved effective in engaging both special and general education students in their learning.

THINK "DIFFERENT," NOT "DISABLED" LEARNER

There is a well-established link between teacher perception and student achievement. View each of your students as an individual with his or her own unique set of strengths and weaknesses. The disability label that is attached to a student with special needs is an administrative convenience rather than an accurate analysis of student need. Put ten students with dyslexia in a special education class and you still have ten different personalities. The only thing they will have in common is their reluctance to read.

While students who are placed in special education programs have learning difficulties, they also have abilities that are overlooked. For years, educators have suspected that some student learning problems have more to do with teaching emphasis than with individual inadequacies. Thinking of students as "different" rather than "disabled" is one of the more powerful ideas to come along in a while. Howard Gardner's (1993) description of multiple intelligence adds teeth to the adage "It's not how smart you are, its how you are smart." The nine forms of intelligence identified by Gardner are visual/spatial, verbal/linguistic, mathematical/ logical, bodily/kinesthetic, musical/ rhythmic, intrapersonal, interpersonal, naturalist, and existentialist. The standard public school curriculum favors students who are strong in verbal/linguistic intelligence over students with strengths in other areas, thus overlooking many student abilities.

In her classic book on learning disabilities *No Easy Answers: The Learning Disabled Child at Home and at School,* Sally Smith (1979), director of the Lab School in Washington, DC, has demonstrated how children can learn when presented with information that matches their preferred learning style. Tom, a young man with dyslexia, was impulsive and uncoordinated. Due to his clumsiness and his propensity to act without thinking, he crashed into desks and knocked materials on the floor. Tom's teacher marked the floor around his desk with wide masking tape on the floor so he could see where "in front of the desk" or "beside the desk" was (emphasis on visual/spatial intelligence). His reading readiness skills were improved by matching loud and soft drum beats to red and yellow poker chips (emphasis on musical/rhythmic intelligence). Dance, drama, filmmaking, music, and graphic arts were all incorporated into Tom's curriculum (emphasis on bodily/kinesthetic intelligence).

Tom is typical of many students who receive special education services. It was not his ability to learn that was impaired. It was his inability to learn through verbal/linguistic teaching methods that hindered his schooling. When teaching methods were expanded to include other intellectual abilities and skills, he succeeded.

While Tom's individual educational program may at first glance seem outside the range of a classroom with 20-plus students, recent research on brain-compatible instruction indicates that all students will perform better when given opportunities to move around, express themselves, and make choices about how they spend their day. Revelations about how the brain processes information indicate the following:

- Movement unites all brain levels and integrates the right and left hemispheres of the neo-cortex. Movement improves memory and helps keep students alert. New information is recalled more efficiently when students are allowed to participate in activities in different areas of the classroom.

- Information is stored in multiple locations throughout the brain and linked in connective networks. Students integrate information and identify patterns through thematic instruction. Integrating curriculum areas such as geometry, geography, and history within a unit on ancient Egypt is more effective than teaching each curriculum area separately.

- The brain quickly discards information it does not perceive as relevant. Connecting aspects of the curriculum to previous learning, personal experiences, life in the community, and personal interests enhances long-term memory.

- The optimum attention span is roughly equivalent in minutes to a student's age in years. Lessons should be brief and broken up into a variety of tasks. For example, a 30-minute lesson could begin with a brief teacher introduction and explanation of learning objectives; 10 minutes of teacher-directed instruction is followed by a 10-minute brainstorming class discussion on how the lesson influences students' daily lives. Finally, students work in cooperative learning groups to summarize key points and produce a 10-question quiz.

- There is a strong connection between emotions and learning. Negative emotions literally shut down thinking ability. On the other hand, positive emotions enhance brain function. Students need positive feedback about their accomplishments rather than negative feedback about their failures. Typical stressors experienced by students include difficulty keeping pace with the curriculum, problems assimilating new information, and trouble following teacher directions.

ORGANIZE COLLABORATIVE LEARNING ACTIVITIES

A main concern of educators within inclusive settings is acceptance of students with disabilities by their peers who were non-disabled. A comprehensive approach is to build cohesiveness through classroom activities that include all students as equal members of the classroom community. Students who engage in collaborative activities on a daily basis come to consider the common good over individual self-interest. Documented benefits of collaborative learning include:

- increased academic performance of at-risk, disabled, and non-disabled students alike.

- enhanced social competence of all students.

- development of conflict-resolution skills.

- development of tolerance for individual differences.

Two useful forms of collaborative learning are cooperative learning and peer tutoring.

Cooperative Learning

Cooperative learning is a successful inclusion strategy for students with mild, moderate, and severe disabilities. More than one hundred studies have documented that students, both disabled and non-disabled, achieve more in cooperative than in competitive learning situations. Johnson and Johnson said, "The average student in a cooperative learning situation performed at approximately the 80th percentile of students in competitive and individualistic learning situations. This finding held for all age groups, ability levels, subject areas, and learning tasks" (Johnson & Johnson, 1986, p. 556).

Cooperative learning infuses democratic procedures into group work. It is appealing to students because they are allowed to socialize and work out their own ideas. Typically, students are put into groups of five or six. Particular attention is given to the effects of group dynamics—specific behaviors that help move the group towards success, the makeup of the group in terms of student strengths and weaknesses, and monitoring to ensure individual accountability. The benefits of cooperative learning are twofold: students are more productive than in ordinary group work, and students practice social skills such as listening, mutual problem solving, and teamwork.

The beneficial effects of cooperative learning embrace all areas of the curriculum. It is an ideal venue for meshing the varied skills and aptitudes of students in elementary and secondary classrooms. Cooperative learning provides a daily routine for revisiting social skills that sustain community ties. The following are basic steps for organizing cooperative learning groups:

- Keep group projects short.

- Frequently change group composition.

- Balance groups for strengths and weaknesses.

- Grade for group work and individual contributions.

- Develop clear rubrics for grades.

- Teach social skills for productive group participation.

- Monitor for group harmony and productivity.

- Build in individual accountability by assigning each member a specific task.

- Assign each person a specific helping role such as "engineer" (keeps the group on track), "counselor" (asks opinions), "reporter" (keeps track of ideas).

- Provide a common stimulus such as a video or group experience.

Peer Tutoring

Peer tutoring is a method for taking advantage of the myriad opportunities each day presents for students to help each other. Both students who are non-disabled and those with disabilities prefer peer tutoring to remedial teacher instruction (Klinger, et. al., 1998). Peer tutoring is the arrangement of students in pairs for instruction. One student—the tutor—does the instructing. The other student—the tutee—is the learner. It is an effective instructional method for all grade levels and subject areas. Peer tutoring improves time on task, lessens distress about errors, enhances motivation, and improves social relationships. Peer tutoring is equally beneficial when students with disabilities tutor non-disabled students and non-disabled students tutor students with disabilities. In the former arrangement, students with disabilities often tutor younger children. Some guidelines for setting up peer tutoring as a regular routine follow:

- Determine the best arrangement for pairing students: cross-age or peer tutoring (see the following section).

- Provide directions on how to tutor, offer feedback, and critique.

- Have regular meetings in which tutors and tutees can discuss how tutoring can be improved.

- Search for ways for both students who are non-disabled and those with disabilities to participate as tutors.

Some variations of the peer tutoring format are class-wide peer tutoring and cross-age peer tutoring. Class-wide peer tutoring (CWPT) involves an entire class in reciprocal teaching. All class members take turns as tutors and tutees. CWPT is recommended as a review strategy, after new material has been introduced and discussed. Cross-age peer tutoring is the systematic tutoring of younger students by older students. This approach is particularly useful with students who are having academic difficulties. Low achieving students get a boost in confidence from helping younger students learn. Additionally, tutoring a younger student helps the tutor review previous concepts that might be problem areas contributing to his or her learning difficulties. The following steps are a guide to establishing a peer tutoring program:

- Start small. Slow development allows for modifications as the tutoring program evolves.

- Prepare students for tutoring. Both tutors and tutees need to know what is expected from them. If students are going to different classrooms, schedules must be balanced, and teachers must agree about specific tutoring objectives. Tutors need clear guidelines about their responsibilities.

- Determine a schedule. Half-hour sessions every day or every other day produce the best results.

- Inform parents. Families are curious about novel teaching methods. Assure parents that tutoring is not depriving students of teacher instruction.

TEACH STRATEGIES FOR EFFICIENT LEARNING

Many students with disabilities need assistance in learning how to learn. The sight of a student bustling late into class without homework and minus his pen and notebook is all too familiar to many teachers. Laments such as "Ashley can't follow directions," "Jerome is always forgetting assignments," and "Jose is so disorganized" underscore how the absence of self-management abilities can impede academic performance. "Learning strategies" is a generic term for a host of interventions designed to help students learn more efficiently. The familiar SQ3R method (Survey, Question, Read, Recite, and Review) has helped students learn to study since the early 1960s. One of the most popular and successful forms of learning strategies is mnemonics. Mnemonics teaches students to "chunk" new information into verbal or visual cues. Karen Sealander (1999) summarizes several mnemonic strategies:

- **HOW** reminds students what a written essay should look like. As with all mnemonics, each letter cues a student to an important step.

  H: Headings that include name, date, subject, and page number.

  O: Organization reminders. For example, start on the front side of the paper and include a left and right margin, and leave at least one blank line at the top and bottom of the page.

  W: Is the paper written neatly?

- **KWL** provides guiding questions to increase comprehension of new information.

  K: What do I already know about the topic?

  W: What do I want to learn?

  L: What have I learned about the new topic?

- **CAPS** helps students identify information in a story.

  C: Who are the characters?

  A: What is the aim of the story?

  P: What problem or situation occurs in the story?

  S: How is the problem solved?

- **TOWER** provides a note taking procedure and a system for drafting essay exams.

  T: Think about the content.

  O: Order the topics.

  W: Write a rough draft.

E: Look for mechanical errors.

R: Revise and rewrite.

Deshler and Shumaker (1986) recommend the following steps for implementing a learning strategy model:

1. Have students make a commitment to the specific learning strategy.

2. Present and describe the learning strategy.

3. Model the strategy and provide practice.

4. Have students verbally rehearse each strategy step.

5. Provide guided practice with feedback.

6. Give positive feedback and generalize the strategy to various academic tasks.

7. Provide maintenance training, support, and feedback.

The notion of guiding students as they cope with tasks can be extended to a variety of problematic situations including attention, time management, homework, critical thinking, and organization. For instance, Hammeken (2000) provides the following suggestions to help students organize their materials and activities:

- Write the daily schedule on the board.

- Color code folders for each subject.

- Provide specific locations in the classroom for daily assignments, late assignments, and take-home materials.

- Stick to the daily classroom routine.

- Allow time for students to share their individual organizational strategies.

- Keep all student supplies in a central area.

- Break up long assignments into shorter units.

- Help students create daily "things-to-do" checklists.

- Enlist parent cooperation in setting specific times for homework.

- Use plastic bags to store writing materials in students' desks.

- Alert students to a change in activities through visual and auditory cues.

- Use graphic organizers to provide a visual overview of specific topics.

MAKE ACCOMMODATIONS

The success of students with special needs in general education classrooms is related to the extent to which teachers are willing to go to provide necessary accommodations. Classroom accommodations take many forms and depend on a number of variables, including type of disability, grade level, and difficulty of material. Also, accommodations need to be implemented in other areas besides instruction. Homework, evaluation of classroom performance, and tests need modifications as well.

The National Center to Improve Tools of Educators (NCITE) recommends six fundamental accommodations to improve the learning of students with disabilities (Burke, Hagan, & Grossen, 1998):

- Use big ideas to help students grasp concepts that cut across various subjects and disciplines. Big ideas are patterns that can be applied in different situations. For example, information can be presented in terms of problem-solution-effect. This rubric can be applied in a multitude of economic, social, political, and scientific situations. For instance, the problem for early colonists was how to support themselves. The solution was slavery. The effect was the Civil War.

- Utilize learning strategies. Explicitly teach problem solving methods. For example, outline how to contribute to a classroom meeting, or specify rubrics for writing an essay.

- Prime background knowledge. Review basic concepts before introducing new information.

- Provide scaffolding. This refers to a steady support system of guidance that can be provided in a variety of ways including a peer tutor, a study guide, interspersed questions, and highlights.

- Offer judicious review. Provide functional situations that require a student to use information in different ways. This helps students generalize skills by allowing them to practice in ways that approximate real-life situations. Read menus, keep track of sports statistics, set up mock stock accounts, hunt for information in the classifieds, and search the Internet. Avoid "drill and kill" reviews such as worksheets. Nothing stifles the desire to learn faster than boring repetition.

- Strategic Integration. Integrate prior learning into more complex ideas. Connect new learning to what a student already knows.

What follows is a sample of accommodations matched to typical student learning problems:

- *Easily distracted.* Learning begins with attention. Look for aspects of the physical environment that can be distracting, such as fluorescent lights flickering, close proximity to the door or window, other students, noise from water pipes, or even the ticking of a clock. Also try parceling assignments into smaller units. Peer tutoring, computer assisted instruction, hands-on activities, and relating tasks to student interest are useful modifications.

- *Difficulty completing tasks.* Give extra time. Shorten assignments and offer praise when work has been completed. Organize tasks so students can have a parallel activity to choose. Allow for different outcomes depending upon ability level. Emphasize correct responses rather than errors. Give alternative assignments. Use visual aids, give concrete examples, and provide hands-on activities. Simplify directions so students are clear on what is expected. Provide an overview of assignments and due dates. Allow students to use learning aids. Sometimes tangible rewards help, but these should be used only as a last resort. The most reinforcing reward for completed work is success. Consider the nature of the task. What invites or discourages participation? Good students find ways to adjust to boring tasks, but problem learners do not. Also, check medications to determine if side effects are hampering student performance.

- *Uncompleted homework.* Communicate with the student's family and request that a specific homework time be established. Have a family member sign each homework assignment. Provide extra credit for homework completed. Use negative reinforcement. For example, homework completed Monday through Thursday earns a reward of no weekend homework. Use homework as a review, not as a method for learning new material. Coordinate with other teachers. The more time homework takes, the less likely it will be completed. Do not use homework as punishment. Provide a homework hotline so students can call each other for help. Set up a homework support Web site or listserv. Provide class time to get started on homework.

- *Difficulty following directions.* Use visual aids. Do not begin directions until all students are ready. Clarify directions by speaking slowly, simplifying vocabulary, checking for understanding, and writing directions on the board. Ask students to repeat the directions. Allow students to work together. Appoint student "teacher aides" to help peers.

- *Disorganized.* Provide students with an assignment notebook. Conduct periodic notebook checks. Provide assignment sheets. Write assignments in the same place on the blackboard. Explain why assignments are necessary. Include a rubric with specific grading criteria. Provide bonus points for good organization. Be organized yourself. Have students keep work in folders. Provide instruction in organizational skills. Encourage students to share organization tips.

- *Gives up easily.* Learned helplessness is a common malady of special education students. Avoid too much one-on-one attention by paraprofessionals. This breeds dependency, and students are clever about getting others to do work for them. Student confidence builds through incremental success. Allow students some choice in their assignments. For example, incorporate learning centers, contracts, and personal goal setting into the classroom. Use media and computer-assisted instruction. Adapt the number of items that a student is supposed to learn. For example, reduce the number of science terms a student is expected to know. Gradually increase the difficulty level of class work. Emphasize effort and give more positive feedback than negative. When grading papers, use green or blue ink rather than red. Use a slash rather than an "X" for wrong answers. Mark the number right out of the total rather than subtracting the number wrong. Keep expectations for success high. Research on teacher perceptions continually demonstrates that how teachers feel about student abilities to a large degree determines academic success.

Assessment, Tests, and Grades

My first special education teaching position was an alternative public school for 45 students with learning and behavior disorders. One of the trickiest problems we teachers had to deal with was grades. Our students had histories of school failure, which included a lengthy series of bad grades. Obviously, we were not going to boost student motivation and self-confidence by grading the same way past teachers had graded. However, inflated grades were not the answer either. After much discussion, we decided to forgo letter and number grades in favor of a rating system for each subject based on "much improved," "improved," and "no improvement." We also thought it would be a good idea for the students to participate in their evaluation process. So before the first marking period, teachers and students met together individually to assess the students' learning.

Both teachers and students gained new insight from this process. Teachers learned how alienated students were from their learning. Some students rebelled. Twelve-year-old Peter said, "It's not my job to decide if I've learned anything; that's your job." Most of the students rated themselves harshly and gave themselves little credit. In the process of accommodating our grading system, we stumbled onto something important: our students felt neither connected to nor responsible for their own learning. Assessment, grades, and tests were something done to them, over which they had no control.

I see this same student reaction as a college professor. Students thank me for "giving an A." One of the most significant accommodations that can be made is to align assessment to learning through curriculum-based assessment. Such curriculum-based materials as student portfolios, scope and sequence checklists, checklists matched to rubrics, samples of student work, student self-evaluations, and criterion-referenced tests provide a much clearer evaluation of progress than do quizzes, norm-referenced tests, and subjective teacher judgments of classroom performance.

Tracking Student Progress

The IEP is a written agreement between the school system and the student's family. It spells out where a student will be placed for special education services, who will deliver the services, any necessary special accommodations, and goals accompanied by a hierarchy of specific behavioral objectives for attaining each goal. The IEP and a school's general curriculum overlap. For a child with multiple disabilities, the IEP might spell out an almost total individualized curriculum; for a student with a mild disability, the IEP will address only those areas where a student is experiencing difficulties, such as mathematics, behavior, or reading.

In areas covered by the IEP, student progress is determined by whether or not a behavioral objective is attained. This criterion-referenced approach to assessment provides an observable measure of progress and builds in teacher accountability. If an objective is not met, teaching methods as well as student traits should be analyzed and necessary adjustments made in the IEP.

An IEP objective contains three elements: condition, behavior, and criteria. The condition spells out the circumstances for evaluating progress, the behavior specifies what the student will do, and the criterion establishes a level of mastery. For example, given a list of 20 multiplication problems (condition), Alex will calculate each with paper and pencil (behavior), with 90% accuracy for three consecutive weeks (criteria). When describing behavior, avoid vague verbs such as "understand," "appreciate," and "learn." Substitute observable verbs such as "calculate," "list," "name," and "sound out."

Periodically collect assessment information to determine if progress is being made towards individual IEP objectives. The condition explains how the student will be assessed, and the criteria set the standard for mastery for the objective. A matrix that lists objectives for each student serves as a useful tracking device. Curriculum-based materials that document each objective can be placed in file folders.

Assessment data increases in value the more frequently it is collected. Daily assessment of student progress provides teachers with feedback needed to determine how well instruction is working. A survey conducted by Zigmond and Miller (1986) found that only 3.5% of special education teachers evaluate progress towards IEP objectives on a daily basis, and only 9.5% collect data on a weekly basis. Absent regular and periodic information about student progress, teachers might incorrectly assume learning is happening, when in fact it is not.

On a visit to a special education classroom, I watched the teacher instruct a group of five students on number concepts. Number cards one through ten were placed sequentially on the eraser tray of a blackboard. Upon request, each student went to the board and pointed to the correct number. The teacher said that they had been doing this drill for a couple of weeks and she was satisfied that the students were able to identify their numbers. I asked if I could move the numbers out of sequence; she agreed, and we repeated the task. Monica was asked to point to the number 7. She went up to the tray, counted off seven cards from left to right and pointed to the number 3. Each student in turn followed the same procedure, and each student pointed to the wrong number. Students develop strategies to disguise learning problems. For this reason, assessment data should be collected in ways that are different from regular classroom instructional routines. Functional assessment is one alternative. Request that students use new skills or information in ways that resemble or model real-life situations.

For example, students can read new vocabulary on a menu, teach a new concept to each other, or do calculations in a mock shopping trip to the grocery store.

Still not resolved to everyone's satisfaction is how to align the general education curriculum with IEPs so students with disabilities will pass mandated state achievement tests. For students with severe disabilities, most states are leaning towards alternative assessments such as curriculum portfolios that document through photos, checklists, and work samples. Students with learning disabilities, emotional disturbance, and mild mental retardation are expected to participate in mandated statewide assessments. Testing accommodations are required by law and need to be considered carefully in order to ensure that each student has the supports he or she needs. Each state is grappling in its own way to ensure the success of students within the climate of standards-based reform and high-stakes testing (tests that students must pass to receive a high school diploma). As these discussions continue, it is critical that inclusive classroom teachers voice their opinions and get involved in decisions that will determine their success as educators.

Testing Accommodations

The 1997 amendments to the Individuals with Disabilities Education Act (IDEA) require that students with disabilities be included in district and statewide assessments. Figure 5.2 provides a list of specific testing accommodations. These accommodations are mandated by law for routine classroom tests as well as standardized tests. Specific accommodations for testing individual students should be included in the IEP to ensure that a student has the same accommodations when taking state-mandated

Figure 5.2

Testing Accommodations

Contents of tests should not be altered; accommodations apply to test administration only.

- Segment tests into shorter time periods.

- Space testing over several days.

- Pick the best time of day to administer a test.

- Use enlarged print for visual difficulties.

- Use praise to reinforce perseverance.

- Allow extra time.

- Provide a scribe.

- Allow students to use a computer.

- List multiple choice questions vertically rather than horizontally.

- Use uncluttered test forms.

- Teach test-taking strategies.

- Allow students to practice with accommodations.

- Provide a reader.

- Use alternate test formats, such as oral tests, allowing use of a scribe, or allowing untimed tests.

- Review tests with students to identify test-taking difficulties.

- Provide rubrics for essay tests to give students concrete writing guidelines.

achievement tests. Examples are listed, but each situation presents different possibilities, so confer with families of affected students for suggestions.

Grading Accommodations

The grading of students with disabilities is contentious. It raises a host of questions, including: what is the purpose of grades, why should grades be adjusted, should effort be graded, and do grades support better learning? Teachers voice a range of opinions about grading special needs students, from grading all students the same to modifying grades to take into account a student's disability.

According to Bradley and Calvin (1998) effective grades should:

1. Be derived from frequent assessments.

2. Include products, progress, and work habits.

3. Accurately convey achievement to parents and students.

4. Give useful feedback that provides the student with direction. (p. 26)

Grading needs to take into account the different traits of students with disabilities. Some specific suggestions for leveling the playing field for all students—those with and those without disabilities—are as follows:

- Base grades on combined assessment of both regular and special education teachers.

- To avoid increasing competition between students, do not post grades.

- Use a variety of curriculum-based assessment approaches to determine grades.

- Develop scoring rubrics that spell out standards for grading.

- Include effort but do not understate achievement.

- Utilize contract grading. Students and teachers determine together quantity and quality required to achieve a specific grade.

- Use IEP objectives as well as the general curriculum as a grading framework.

- If a test includes various types of questions (multiple choice, essay, short answer, etc.), grade each section separately. This helps to determine the type of test item that best suits a student's abilities.

- Base grades on satisfactory completion of modified assignments.

- Provide opportunities for extra credit.

- Do not penalize students for learning inadequacies directly related to their disabilities (for example, if a student with dyslexia does not complete the required reading assignment).

- Look for recurring errors and avoid penalizing a student for the same repeated mistake (for example, a third grade teacher marks a math paper with a zero because all the math calculations are wrong, even though the student has made the same miscalculation on every problem).

Clearly, grades must be consistent with school policy, but grades must also reflect attainment of IEP goals and objectives.

Including grading accommodations within a student's IEP provides families of students with disabilities with a clear picture of how their child will be evaluated.

BALANCE DIRECT INSTRUCTION WITH GUIDED INQUIRY

It is fitting to conclude this chapter on instruction with a discussion of one of American education's longest running feuds about the best way to teach. In one camp there are those who base their claims on direct instruction. In the other camp are those who base their claims on guided inquiry.

Direct instruction is teacher-directed and is characterized by the following sequence:

1. Review and check previous work (re-teach if necessary).

2. Group presentation of new content/skills.

3. Guided practice.

4. Feedback and correction.

5. Independent practice.

6. Weekly and monthly reviews.

Examples of direct instruction include phonological instruction, effective instruction, precision teaching, programmed learning, mastery learning, and behavior modification. Critics of direct instruction claim it is rigid and boring. Advocates of direct instruction claim it is scientific and the best way to prepare students for standardized tests.

Guided inquiry is student-centered and structured.

Students are encouraged to develop their own unique ideas through some of the following procedures:

1. Providing students with choices.

2. Encouraging students to share their perceptions.

3. Emphasizing independent thinking rather than "right" and "wrong" answers.

4. Focusing on direct experience with materials rather than paper and pencil work.

5. Providing opportunities for students to see the functional connections between academic disciplines.

6. Organizing collaborative learning tasks.

Examples of guided inquiry include cooperative learning, peer tutoring, learning centers, whole language, open education, learning strategies, and constructivism. Critics of guided inquiry claim it is unfocused and lacks standards. Advocates of guided inquiry claim it matches student developmental needs and encourages critical thinking.

So who is right? Which group of prospectors is mining the real stuff and which group is holding fool's gold? The answer, as most experienced teachers know, is that both are valuable (Algozzine & Maheady, 1986). There are nuggets and fool's gold in both camps. Despite its many documented successes, direct instruction can be tedious and literally drive students to distraction. Although it can count luminaries such as John Dewey among its advocates, guided instruction can be so disorganized that activities degenerate into chaos. The unifying principle that brings out the best in each approach is presenting a lesson in a way that captures student interest. If students lack motivation to participate, no instructional approach, no matter how elegant, is going to succeed.

Despite researchers' best efforts to create scientific "teacher proof" instructional methods, teaching is first and foremost a human relations job. I frequently ask my education major undergraduates to describe their "best" teachers. Rarely is a specific instructional approach mentioned. These prospective educators describe teachers who touched them personally through their enthusiasm, challenges, and caring. When children enter kindergarten, they are perpetual learning machines—you cannot shut them down. As time goes by, they lose their spark and learning becomes a chore. Only in school is learning called "work."

Motivating teachers search for ways to rekindle the joy of learning. They are energetic and positive about learning. They smile at their students and share their humor. They care about their subject matter and spend time outside of school boning up on new developments in their field. Motivating teachers search for ways to make their instruction relevant. They tie ideas to students' lives and interests. Motivating teachers recognize that every student has the capability to learn and they understand that the greatest disservice is to lower expectations.

A balance of direct instruction with guided discovery injects novelty into classroom activities. It keeps both teachers and students on their toes. Most of all, a combination of instructional approaches helps teachers determine which approach is most effective with specific students. A balance of instructional approaches—part direct instruction and part guided inquiry—individualizes education, and that is what special education is all about.

Chapter 6

Managing Student Behavior

MANAGING PROBLEM BEHAVIORS IS A PRIMARY CONCERN within inclusive classrooms. Effective discipline requires flexibility. No single approach to classroom management can possibly meet the diverse needs presented by special education students. There is an old saying, "If the only tool you have is a hammer, you will deal with every problem as if were a nail." Like skilled carpenters, inclusive teachers must be able to select the appropriate behavior management tool to deal with a specific situation.

Changing one's own behavior is difficult; attempting to change another's behavior is formidable. Direct attempts to change another individual are usually met with resentment and resistance. For many years, behavior modification was the preferred approach to managing behavior problems presented by special education students. The emphasis was on controlling student behavior through systematic application of rewards and punishment. Behavior modification techniques, used appropriately, can be a useful tool for some behavior situations. However, overuse of rewards and punishment places too much emphasis on controlling student behavior and not enough emphasis on teaching students to control their own behavior.

Less than 25% of special education students with identified emotional or behavioral problems are placed in regular classrooms (Department of Education, 2001). Many of these students are placed in special education programs not because of severe emotional problems but because of chronic school discipline infractions. Impulsivity, hyperactivity, noncompliance, and conflicts with authority are the most common behavior complaints that generate special education referrals. Often poor or raised in unstable homes, these children have few advocates.

Meanwhile, mental health experts fear that students with more severe emotional problems are overlooked because they do not present a classroom nuisance. Placed in self-contained special education classes or alternative schools, these students drop off the education horizon. Separate education programs for students with emotional and behavioral problems are the least successful of any special education enterprise (Knitzer, et al., 1990). Once placed in these programs, few students return to regular education. They drop out of school at a rate of 50%—twice the national rate. Employment options are marginal and arrests within a few years of leaving school are common. In this era of No Child Left Behind, students with problem behaviors are education's throwaway kids.

Avoid placement in separate special education programs by supporting students with problem behaviors in the regular classroom. This is accomplished by using classroom interventions that have a solid empirical track record. Analysis of over 800 studies on effective classroom management has documented the success of the following strategies for students with problem behaviors (U.S. Department of Education, 2000):

1. Behaviorally-based interventions that combine encouragement with consistent responses to both positive and negative actions.

2. Quality academic instruction.

3. Social skill instruction.

FOCUS ON BEHAVIOR SOLUTIONS, NOT ON BEHAVIOR PROBLEMS

Managing behavior problems in an inclusive classroom can best be accomplished by recognizing that all misbehavior happens for a reason. This interactional view of behavior is represented by the formula $B = f(E \times I)$: Behavior is a function of the environment times the individual (Hall, Lindzey, & Campbell, 1998, p. 325). When confronted with problem behavior, some teachers focus their attention solely on the student, and in the process overlook contributing classroom conditions. Miguel keeps talking out of turn, so the teacher moves his assigned seat in front of her. Alexis will not stop fidgeting, so the teacher puts her out in the hall. Jerome refuses to finish his assignment, so he is sent to the principal's office. All of these attempts at behavior change assume the student is in complete control of his or her behavior and is simply choosing to be a nuisance.

The interactional view, first articulated by the noted psychologist Kurt Lewin (1936), presents another explanation: Behavior is influenced by the combination of individual temperament and environmental conditions. Temperament includes a student's developmental history, perceptions, neurological status, and personality. Environment encompasses daily routines, instructional methods, teacher behavior, physical arrangement of the classroom, and peer influence. Student behavior can be changed by making environmental adjustments. The following questions posed by Daniels (1998) provide a practical framework for analyzing interactional conditions that contribute to behavior problems:

- Could the misbehavior be a result of inappropriate curriculum or teaching strategies?

- Could the misbehavior be a result of the student's inability to understand the concepts being taught?

- Could the misbehavior be an underlying result of a student's disability?

- Could physical conditions be contributing to the misbehavior (for example, room temperature, flickering lights, students' remaining seated for long periods of time, the physical arrangement of furniture, etc.)?

- Could the student's temperament be a contributing factor (is she bored, easily frustrated, impulsive)?

- Which of the above factors can I control? Which of the above factors do I need support in order to address—either parental, administrative, professional, or a combination of these supports?

- What is the best way to help students to self-manage their behavior? (Would a specific social skills program help?)

- How could reinforcement strategies (positive reinforcement, negative reinforcement, intermittent reinforcement) be used to help manage behavior?

- Is it appropriate to use punishment, and what are the unintended consequences of punishment?

Teach Consequences; Don't Punish

Punishment and threats are two of the most common behavior interventions used in schools. Consider that, despite longstanding criticism from virtually every major education organization, corporal punishment is still practiced in 23 states. No American psychologist has had a greater influence on the development of behaviorally based interventions than B. F. Skinner. Skinner was convinced that punishment was an ineffective tool for changing human behavior. The trouble with punishment, according to Skinner, is that it causes resentment and it does not teach new behaviors. Experts in behavior modification point out that punishment should be used only if it decreases a specific behavior. If a student continues to engage in behaviors for which she has been punished, then clearly punishment is not effective and should be abandoned as a behavior intervention.

Punishment and threats seem to fix a problem because they often stop misbehavior in its tracks. Samuel stops clowning around when his teacher threatens loss of recess. After a scolding, Marie sits up straight. Jorge is sent to the principal's office because he didn't follow the teacher's instructions. In each situation, the offensive student behavior ceases after the punishment. This result encourages the teacher to use punishment again. This is a fine example of negative reinforcement. The aversive student behavior is eliminated by punishment, thus the punishing behavior is reinforced.

With these kinds of results, the reader might be asking at this point, "What's the problem?" Simply put, in the majority of cases, particularly with students who have chronic discipline problems, the cessation of misbehavior is temporary. Within a short time, Samuel will start clowning around again, Marie will slouch in her seat, and Jorge will not listen to his teacher. If you are skeptical, accept the "data challenge." For a week, count the number of times a student engages in a typical misbehavior. Administer the usual punishments. Then, a month later, do a re-count and see if the misbehavior has decreased. Teachers who use punishment or threats of punishment as their primary means of halting misbehavior get short-term results that offer relief, but there is no long-term change in student behavior. Nor does the student learn constructive social skills to supplant misbehavior.

Punishments and threats work best with students who are infrequent behavior problems. Within inclusion programs, a teacher will encounter students who need more sophisticated behavior interventions. Many students with behavior problems have a lengthy punishment history and still their difficulties persist.

Miguel attended an alternative high school. The 17-year-old was known for his quick wit and impulsive behavior. A day after returning to the school from a 30-day stint in a youth detention center, Miguel met with the school counselor. The counselor and Miguel discussed some ideas for making school a better place for him.

He enjoyed working with younger students, so the counselor helped arrange with his teachers for him to begin doing some peer tutoring. During their discussion, Miguel vowed he would never do anything again that would get him sent back to the detention center. Two days later, he made sexual advances to a female student in class. He was removed from the classroom and in the process he got into an argument with his teacher. The principal suspended him. Because suspension was a probation violation, Miguel was remanded to the juvenile detention center for two more weeks.

Punishment does not have the desired effect with students like Miguel because they fail to consider consequences before they act (Henley & Long, 1999). Persistent offenders view punishment as retribution rather than as a logical consequence for misbehavior. They develop cognitive distortions to justify their behavior. For example, a common misperception among chronic offenders is that victims bring their troubles on themselves. A car is stolen because the driver left the keys in the ignition, or a student is beaten up because he was in the wrong place at the wrong time. When chronic offenders are caught, they blame "bad luck." These students are first-class manipulators. They have refined this skill through the habitual process of rationalizing their deeds to themselves and others. These students do not understand the difference between punishment and consequences. This distinction is an important one, and the re-education can begin within inclusive classrooms.

Punishment is often delivered in anger and the connection between offense and penalty is weak. The following are punishments:

- Raul refuses to do work and his teacher sends him to the principal's office.

- Franklin bullies a classmate in the cafeteria and he is given a week of detention.

- Janine leaves the classroom without permission, and her teacher assigns extra math homework.

Consequences are presented without anger and there is a link between action and result. The following are consequences:

- Raul refuses to do schoolwork, so he has to complete the assignment during free time.

- Franklin bullies a classmate in the cafeteria, so he has to eat alone in the classroom for a week.

- Janine leaves the classroom without permission, so she cannot use a hall pass for two days.

Consequences establish a logical connection between behavior and sanction. Allowing students to participate in establishing behavioral guides and sanctions at the beginning of the school year helps students learn to be accountable for their behavior. Over a period of time, consequences that are logically tied to mutually agreed upon behavior guidelines can help teach students the social skills they need for successful classroom participation. However, logical consequences are only part of the solution. Peer groups have a powerful influence on individual behavior. Indeed, it is the quest for peer acceptance that drives students to indulge in such dangerous behaviors as early sex, drinking, drugs, and smoking. Successful inclusion teachers promote the development of positive peer relationships.

BUILD A STUDENT SUPPORT NETWORK

The survival of a democratic society rests on the willingness of its citizens to accept and embrace individual differences. The inclusive classroom does not simply teach diversity—it is diversity in action. The mingling of students with disabilities and those without can provide real-life lessons in how everyone, regardless of appearance or talent, has the potential to contribute. If these lessons are to take hold, however, it is necessary to provide a structure that promotes student affiliations. Without orchestration, students who are non-disabled often ignore or reject students with disabilities.

Monda-Amaya and Pavri (2001) reported that even though included in the regular classroom, students with learning disabilities felt lonely. The tendency to avoid personal contact with special education students becomes more pronounced through middle and high school years. Three common situations that diminish relationships among students are that students are physically integrated into the classroom but are placed apart from other students and not included in group work; students with disabilities are treated like "mascots" and taken care of by other students; and students are treated well in the classroom, but rejected or neglected outside of the classroom.

Some ways to help develop peer relations among students include:

- During the first weeks of school, have students interview and introduce each other to the class.

- Highlight shared values and traditions.

- Model, support, and praise considerate behaviors.

- Show videos that feature individuals with disabilities and follow with class discussions.

- Organize disability simulation activities.

- Help students who are non-disabled pick up on gesture cues from students who are nonverbal.

- Support extracurricular school activities that integrate students.

- Develop activities to increase student interactions during recess and meal times.

- Keep track of spontaneous student interactions and duplicate conditions that promote those interactions.

- Have honest conversations with the entire class about modifications that some students need in their routines and assignments.

- Assign classroom "buddies" for new student orientation.

- Discuss current events that center on individuals with disabilities.

- Survey students about what they like and do not like about school.

PRACTICE PREVENTIVE DISCIPLINE

The majority of classroom behavior problems are minor disruptions that interfere with the flow of normal routines. A bored student's whispering distracts students sitting around him. A frustrated student's complaining irritates her teacher. An angry student refuses to complete an assignment. Over the course of a

5-hour day, events such as these add up to hundreds of incidents that interfere with learning. The following preventive discipline techniques can significantly reduce classroom disruptions and increase responsible student behavior.

Provide Activity-Based Learning

Four of the most common classroom instructional methods—reading from a textbook, completing worksheets, listening to the teacher lecture, and writing notes—discourage learning because they require minimal student participation. The more senses a student uses to complete a lesson, the more attentive that student will be. Activities that require students to move around, voice their opinions, discuss ideas with other students, and use their emotions enhance learning by engaging multiple areas of the brain. Movement focuses attention and integrates cognitive areas of the brain. Lessons that include tactile manipulation of materials stimulate learning because the skin is linked to more brain neurons than is any other organ. The limbic system of the brain links emotions to the neocortex—the thinking part of the brain. Lessons that prompt emotional responses such as empathy, surprise, and humor enhance recall. Activities that link new knowledge to direct experience are more easily incorporated into existing student thought patterns.

Move Around the Room

Proximity encourages constructive behavior. Teachers who stay rooted to the front of the room create a spatial and emotional gap between themselves and their students. Physical proximity creates a sense of intimacy. Teachers who stay rooted to the front of the classroom deal with student behavior through corrective verbal comments. These comments draw attention to misbehavior and disrupt the flow of classroom activities. There should be no front or back to a classroom. Put the teacher's desk to the side and use all the classroom space for walking and teaching.

Establish Smooth Transitions

Changing activities from one class to another or from one activity to another requires planning. Sometimes students walk into class upset about something that happened during recess or in the hall. Within the classroom, there are always a few students who cannot locate their materials or need more directions. Alerting students that a change is coming, clearly posting schedules, and preparing teaching materials ahead of time can eliminate some transition disturbances. However, expect the unexpected. Students who are upset need time and a place to calm down. Students who have attention problems need directions printed simply and clearly on the board. Students who are constantly forgetting assignments or losing materials need organizational props such as assignment books, color-coded binders, and knapsacks. Keep in mind that movement is noisy. It is not necessary to attend to every minor disruption—Fritz Redl (1952) called this "planned ignoring." Use common sense when students are upset or excited.

Don't Take Misbehavior Personally

Teachers have specific behaviors that annoy them. When the educational organization Phi Delta Kappa asked teachers to rank student behaviors they found most offensive, teachers listed schoolwork not completed, behavior that disrupts the class, and disobedience. The number one reason teachers leave the profession is discipline problems (Langdon, 1996). The problems cited are more personal than issues of normal classroom decorum. Frequent complaining, name calling, and untidiness are examples of some student behaviors that irritate teachers. When dealing with misbehavior, it is important to acknowledge sensitivity to specific actions. Otherwise, one runs the risk of reacting in an impulsive and angry manner.

Teachers need to model the social behaviors they want to nurture in their students. When teachers react in anger to unpleasant behavior the subliminal message they send to their students is that it is okay to yell, punish, or humiliate. Ironically, students with behavior and emotional problems, who seem lacking in empathy, are often very perceptive about teacher pet peeves. It is almost as though some teachers walk around with big buttons pinned to their chests that say "push me." These metaphorical buttons are invisible to the teachers, but plain to students. Know your pet peeves and understand how vital it is to react to student behavior in a calm and measured way. Long and Morse (1996) have reported that while students usually initiate conflict situations in school, the majority of serious behavioral confrontations are the result of teacher over-reaction to minor classroom disturbances.

Search for Causes of Misbehavior

Researchers at the Phi Delta Kappa Commission on Discipline (1982) conducted a national survey of schools with effective discipline practices. A common characteristic in each of the surveyed schools was the value placed on solutions rather than punishment. When confronted with serious behavior problems such as racial tensions, student apathy, and vandalism, staff adopted a problem solving approach. They interviewed students, discussed options, and put into place programs to build a more positive learning environment. Administrators at Wyatt High School in Fort Worth, Texas, brought leaders of different student groups together to talk, listen, and work out solutions to racial tensions together. A weekend retreat helped change student attitudes. Teachers and administrators at Eagle Grove High School in Eagle Grove, Iowa, identified lack of interest and lack of school spirit as symptoms of student apathy. A tightening of school policies along with increased parental involvement brought about a positive change in student attitude. Educators at the RCA School Youth Development Center in Cornwall Heights, Pennsylvania, identified racism as a contributor to vandalism. The problem was solved by establishing a policy of allowing students to share power and authority with administrators and teachers.

There is always a reason for misbehavior. The rush to punish offenders overlooks causes and does nothing to change behavior patterns. Some typical examples—students fooling around in class, for example—are often linked to mundane lessons and irrelevant curriculum; "grandstanding" and other attention-seeking behavior is often an attempt to garner peer acceptance; unwillingness to do schoolwork is common among special education students who associate school with consistent failure. Interesting lessons enhance student involvement. Classroom activities that recognize student attributes diminish acting out behavior. Academic accomplishment supported by carefully orchestrated successes incrementally builds student interest in schoolwork.

Use Humor

Mr. Davis was a permanent substitute teacher in an inner-city elementary school. His job was to fill in for any teacher who was absent on a particular day. He worked the entire range of grades, from kindergarten to sixth. One day he was assigned to a difficult fourth grade class. Several students in the class were well known throughout the school as frequent rule breakers. Chief among these was Michael—a gawky 9-year-old with a wide grin and a penchant for mischief. Mr. Davis had no sooner walked into the class at 9:00 a.m. when his troubles began. Edna said she had to go to the bathroom, but the pass was nowhere in sight. The students pounced on this problem en masse. Some jumped out of their seats and began searching the room; others argued among themselves about possible places the pass could be located. Still others shouted out advice. Mr. Davis realized that unless he quickly ended the clamor he would spend his entire day just trying to maintain control. He spotted Michael sitting on his desk observing the melee. A look of contentment spread across Michael's face. Mr. Davis asked Michael to come to the front of the room and hold out his hand. With a washable marker, Mr. Davis wrote "PASS" on Michael's palm. "Michael," he said, "You are the official 'pass' for the day." This delighted the class, and Michael as well. He smiled and said, "I'm the pass and I don't want any fooling around." The class settled into their daily routine and Michael performed his new role admirably.

Humor eases tension and is one of the best ways to defuse behavior problems. When humor is defined as telling jokes and silly anecdotes, few teachers would consider themselves humorous. But humor is more a state of mind than a series of one-liners. Humorous teachers are those who smile, poke fun at themselves, and look for the up side to daily routines. Humor is not sarcasm or jokes made at the expense of individuals. Good humor is listening to students, appreciating frivolity, and making each student feel that he or she is a worthwhile person.

Give Students Responsibilities

Nothing helps build a trusting relationship and positive behavior more effectively than students' belief that their teacher has faith in them. Responsibility is learned, not earned. Teachers who allow only the "good" students to carry messages and do small tasks, such as pass out papers, use responsibility as a reward rather than as a teaching tool. In order to be responsible, students need practice.

Classroom responsibilities should not be given or taken away based on good comportment. When students make a mistake or get into trouble, they need the opportunity to prove themselves capable. A good baseball coach does not take a player out of a game because of an error on the field. Keep students "in the game" by highlighting their contributions, not their mistakes.

Look around your classroom, survey your daily routines, ask students their opinion about tasks with which they could help. Some examples of regular routines students can take care of are taking attendance, carrying messages, tutoring, watering plants, decorating the room, making copies, orienting new students, passing out materials, making classroom announcements, leading brainstorming sessions, working on committees, and making phone calls.

Remember that students who are prone to misbehavior are barraged with negative comments about their actions and their negative effect on others. Classroom responsibilities provide positive offsetting experiences that build self-confidence and carry prestige among peers.

TEACH SOCIAL SKILLS

A growing body of research indicates that children who enter public school with a minimum of social skills are at great risk of school failure (Brigman, Lane, & Switzer, 1999). As Daniel Goleman noted in his best-selling book *Emotional Intelligence* (1995), the ability to work well with others is a crucial determinant for success. Key elements in emotional intelligence are empathy, self-control, and maintaining relationships. These are areas in which students with disabilities experience difficulties. Disruptive student behavior and ostracism by peers are serious obstacles to successful inclusion programs.

Many students with special needs enter school without the social skills they need to control their behavior and relate to peers. Some lack appropriate social skills because they have a neurological or metabolic problem that interferes with their social development. There was a time when a neurological deficit seemed a permanent disability with little hope for recovery. However, recent neurological research indicates that given appropriate environmental stimulation, mental pathways re-organize themselves into new and more efficient transmitters of information (Diamond & Hopson, 1998; Sylwester, 2000). The reconfiguration of neural pathways progresses as students practice new social behaviors.

Some students have not been taught appropriate social skills at home or in their community. Before age five, children need to observe the significant adults in their lives modeling appropriate social skills. A youngster who grows up in a home where feelings are acted out instead of discussed will adapt to that pattern of behavior. After age five, the influence of peers grows. By the time a child reaches adolescence, peers have overtaken family members as models. Poverty-stricken communities in particular, either rural or urban, are high-risk environments for young people. They will adapt. Young people are genetically wired to survive; quick action and aggressiveness may serve a useful purpose on the streets, but will likely lead to trouble in school.

Other children have not had ample time to practice appropriate social skills. They can describe and discuss how to behave, but they cannot spontaneously put their knowledge to use. Like golfers who read articles on how to hit a strong drive down a narrow fairway, these students know what to do, but when it comes to performance, they fall short. The unpracticed student can be particularly frustrating to teachers because he knows what to do but still gets it wrong.

Social skill instruction might seem an additional burden to hard-pressed teachers, but it actually goes on all the time. Every time a teacher establishes a rule, talks with a student about behavior, or organizes students to work together, she is teaching social skills. However, this incidental social skill instruction is unfocused in terms of assessment of student strengths and weaknesses, selection of appropriate skills for instruction, and teaching methods.

There are many published social skill curricula available that provide a guide for social skill instruction. Published programs differ in terms of specific skills addressed and teaching methods employed. Each program includes its own version of core social skills, methods for assessing student progress, and specific teaching methods. For example, *Teaching Self-Control: A Curriculum for Responsible Behavior* (Henley, 2003) focuses specifically on 20 skills that comprise control. The skills are organized into five areas: impulse control, stress management, group participation, social problem solving, and following school routines. Teaching methods emphasize integration of social skill instruction with the academic curriculum. Table 6.1 lists some social skill programs that are useful for inclusion programs.

When selecting a social skill program, consider the following questions:

- Is the program research-based?

- Does the curriculum provide a reliable method for assessing student social skill abilities?

- Are teaching methods compatible with classroom routines?

- Is the program flexible?

Some authors, for example Alfie Kohn (1997), eschew published social skill curricula. Kohn believes that published curricula stifle the natural development of key human values. In lieu of packaged programs, Kohn recommends that teachers develop a caring community. In Kohn's view, students become responsible when they make important decisions about classroom events that affect them. Specific social skills that reflect Kohn's caring focus include cooperation, peer relationships, and conflict management. Like several other authors, Kohn believes that classrooms should reflect the democratic principles that we hold so dear in society at large. One advantage of Kohn's community approach is that all the activities of the day present opportunities to support student social skill development. In contrast, some published social skill curricula isolate part of the day for social skill instruction. Treating social skill development as a solitary subject like math or science overlooks the multitude of possibilities each day

Table 6.1

Social Skills Programs

Anti-bias Curriculum: Tools for Empowering Young Children. (1989) By Louise Derman-Sparks. National Association for the Education of Young Children.

Bully Proofing Your School: A Comprehensive Approach for Elementary Schools. (1994) By Carla Garrity, Kathryn Jens, William Porter, Nancy Sager, & Cam Short-Camilli. Sopris West.

The Bullying Prevention Handbook: A Guide for Principals, Teachers, and Counselors. (1996) By John Hoover and Ronald Oliver. National Educational Service.

Connecting with Others: Lessons for Teaching Social and Emotional Competence. (1996) By Rita C. Richardson. Research Press.

Developmental Therapy—Developmental Teaching (Third Edition). (1996) By Mary Wood, Karen Davis, Faye Swindle, & Constance Quirk. Pro-Ed Press.

Energies and Icebreakers. (1989) By Elizabeth Foster. Educational Media Corporation.

The Equip Program: Teaching Youth to Think and Act Responsibly Through a Peer-Helping Approach. (1995) By John Gibbs, Granville Bud Potter, and Arnold Goldstein. Research Press.

Teaching Self-Control: A Curriculum for Responsible Behavior (Second Edition). (2003) By Martin Henley. National Educational Service.

Tribes: A New Way of Learning and Being Together. (1995) By Jeanne Gibbs. Center Source Publications.

Tribes: A Process for Social Development and Cooperative Learning. (1987) By Jeanne Gibbs. Center-Source Publications.

offers to teach students how to manage their own emotions and relate more effectively with others.

Some teaching methods that support social skill instruction are:

- *Modeling.* Teachers need to demonstrate the social skills they want to foster within their students. Every teacher-student exchange has a classroom audience. Teachers who preach respect and then make negative comments when students misbehave are poor models and are unlikely to convince students of the value of mutual respect.

- *Cooperative learning.* There is more to cooperative learning than putting students into a group to complete an assignment. Students need to be taught such group process skills as questioning, listening, compromising, and accountability. They also need to understand that there are specific behaviors, such as monopolizing and going off on a tangent, that interfere with group communication. Role playing and brainstorming are two methods of introducing students to the specific skills they need in order to be productive group participants. Practice helpful group roles and provide students with feedback about their participation within groups.

- *Class meetings.* Class meetings provide regular forums for student discussion. They need to be structured to maximize participation and limit negative interactions such as students putting down other students' ideas. Begin by having students brainstorm discussion guidelines for talking and listening. Agree on a topic and have students practice in pairs. Have each student report on what the other student had to say. Proceed into large group discussions when students seem ready. Always begin with an agenda and adhere to discussion rules. Establish a time limit.

- *Choice.* Providing students with choices increases their sense of ownership of their behavior. Students need some control over events that affect them. When students lack constructive ways of gaining some control over their lives, they will continue to strive to have this basic human need met through unconstructive behavior (for example, refusing to finish work, or truancy). Some ways teachers can involve students in decision making include decorating the classroom, selecting between two activities, helping develop classroom rules, making decisions about fund raising and community service, presenting the parts of the curriculum and asking students where they would like to begin, using brainstorming as an instructional technique, and surveying students about their likes, dislikes, and school-based concerns.

Social skill instruction does not provide a quick fix for behavior problems. Just as mathematics and reading are long-term projects, so is social skill development. However, when social skill instruction is incorporated into daily classroom routines, behavior change is often accompanied by improved academic performance.

Chapter 7

What's In It for Me?

THE READER OF A GOOD NOVEL EAGERLY ANTICIPATES the last chapter. It is the final installment of a story that has held the reader's attention for hundreds of pages. Sad, happy, or surprising — whatever the conclusion, it is the capstone of a worthwhile journey. With education books, the last chapter is more often approached with a sigh of relief as in — "I'm almost done!" This is not how the author wants things to end. Rather, the writer's hope is to send the reader off armed with vivid ideas and bold plans of action. Too often, however, in casting about for something significant to say, the writer settles for a summary and few upbeat aphorisms. For the writer of nonfiction, the last chapter is the most difficult because he or she, like the reader, yearns to finish, yet the nagging belief that there is still something important to say refuses to go away.

LOOK FOR BENEFITS

Having provided a series of recommendations on legal principles, behavior management strategies, instructional accommodations, and administrative priorities that gird successful inclusion programs, I would be remiss if I did not point out one final point: good inclusion programs benefit everyone. Students with disabilities are neither more nor less important than the rest of the students. Successful inclusion programs do not sacrifice the learning of non-disabled students. When approached about the prospect of teaching in an inclusive classroom, a teacher has a responsibility to ask, "What's in it for me and my students?" The phrasing should be more diplomatic, but the question needs to be asked. The answer will speak volumes about the reliability of administrative support and educational resources.

Resources provided to special education students can be used to enhance the quality of instruction for students who are non-disabled as well. A special education teacher assigned to an inclusive classroom might work with small groups of students who are disabled and non-disabled. Paraprofessionals can be used in a similar fashion. Equipment such as additional computers can be shared by all students. Benefits accrue when regular classroom teachers are allowed to make decisions about how additional resources are managed. When researchers asked regular education teachers if they would like to be part of an inclusion program, the majority said no. When the question was rephrased so teachers could choose their own classroom modifications, 54% said yes (Myles & Simpson, 1989). Clearly, many regular education teachers are up to the task of inclusive education, and they understand the necessity of matching efforts with resources.

McLesky and Waldron (1996) have helped establish successful inclusion programs throughout the country. About benefits for all students they write:

One of the criticisms to inclusion in many schools is that too much is being made of the needs of one small group of students. We agree with this statement if inclusion only benefits students with disabilities. Rather, a primary goal of inclusion should be to allow teachers in general education classrooms to better meet the needs of all students. This will most likely include not only those with disabilities but also slow learners, students who are perceived to be at risk of school failure, students who learn curriculum quickly and become bored, students with attentional problems and so forth. Improved instruction, a curriculum that is more child centered, collaboration with other teachers to address student problems, and a range of other features of inclusive classrooms should allow this objective to be met. (p. 152)

Increased resources for all students shifts intervention efforts from remediation to prevention.

PREVENT RATHER THAN REMEDIATE

Remedial special education interventions such as self-contained classrooms and pull-out programs have a dubious track record for students with academic and emotional disabilities. These students drop out of school at double the rate of other students. Unemployment and incarceration rates of these special education students are significantly higher than those of their peers (Bullis, Yovanoff, Mueller, & Havel, 2002). Students with academic and emotional disabilities account for 80% of the entire special education population. Most are not identified as requiring special education services until they begin encountering difficulties in the regular classroom. Inclusion offers the possibility of preventing learning problems from escalating to the point where special education is needed. A special education teacher who is stationed in a regular classroom for at least part of the school day could work with students who are at risk by:

- providing additional reading instruction using multi-sensory materials.

- establishing a social skills intervention program that meshes with the academic curriculum.

- directly teaching learning strategies to students with attentional and organizational difficulties.

- developing positive behavioral supports for students who present a discipline problem.

- monitoring student progress using criterion-referenced learning objectives.

The average cost of a special education evaluation is $500. The cost of educating a special education student is twice that of educating a non-special education student. A student placed in an alternative special education program can cost a school system $35,000 a year. Over six million students receive special education services nationwide, and the majority of these students have academic or emotional disabilities that surfaced in the regular classroom. Meanwhile, the numbers of students placed in special education programs nationwide increases by about 200,000 every year.

These trends can be reversed. The influx of special education services into the regular classroom offers the possibility of long-term savings. For too long, special and regular educators have traveled on different tracks to get to the same destination. During tough times, parallel educational systems compete for resources; in good times, the best each has to offer is hidden from the other's view. Inclusion melds resources, combines talent, and unifies goals. Properly organized, an inclusion program can enhance classroom resources, stem the tide of special education referrals, and provide an appropriate education for students with disabilities. With so much to gain, why hesitate to move forward?

Leave no child behind is more than a slogan. It is a succinct phrasing of the public school mission. Working together, regular and special educators can achieve more than they can working separately. However, inclusion requires a change in how the business of schooling is conducted, and change can be scary. McLesky and Waldron (1996) suggest that inclusion programs be viewed not as finished products, but as works in progress. This makes good sense. No innovation develops without warts and wrinkles. Mistakes happen and adjustments are made. Trial and error is the handmaiden of progress. Thomas Edison made one thousand unsuccessful attempts at inventing the light bulb. When asked, how it felt to fail one thousand times Edison replied, "I didn't fail one thousand times. The light bulb was an invention with one thousand steps."

References

Algozzine, B., & Maheady, L. (1986). When all else fails, teach! *Exceptional Children, 52*(6), 487–488.

Auden, W. H. (1947). *The age of anxiety: A baroque eclogue.* New York: Random House.

Baker, E. T., Wang, M. C. & Walberg, H. J. (1994). The effects of inclusion on learning. *Educational Leadership, 52*(4), 33–35.

Beattie, J. R., Anderson, R.J., & Antonak, R. F. (1997). Modifying attitudes of prospective educators towards students with disabilities and their integration in regular classrooms. *The Journal of Psychology, 131*, 245–260.

Beck, M., & Malley, J. (1998). The pedagogy of belonging. *Reclaiming Children and Youth: Journal of Emotional and Behavioral Problems, 7*(3), 133–137.

Bennet, T., & DeLuca, D. (1997). Putting inclusion into practice: Perspectives of teachers and parents. *Exceptional Children, 64,* 115–117.

Blatt, B., & Kaplan, F. (1966). *Christmas in purgatory.* Boston: Allyn and Bacon.

Bradley, D. F., & Calvin, M. B. (1998). Grading modified assignments: Equity or compromise? *Teaching Exceptional Children, 31*(2), 24–29.

Brendtro, L. K., Brokenleg, M., & Van Bockern, S. (2001). *Reclaiming youth at-risk: Our hope for the future.* Bloomington, IN: National Educational Service.

Brigman, G., Lane, D., & Switzer, D. (1999, July/August). Teaching students school success skills. *Journal of Educational Research, 92,* 323–327.

Brinker, R. P. (1983). *Why integration for severely handicapped students?* Princeton: Educational Testing Service.

Brophy, J. E., & Good, T. L. (1986). Teacher behavior and student achievement. In M.C. Wittrock (Ed.), *Handbook of research and teaching* (pp. 328–376). New York: Macmillan.

Bullis, M., Yovanoff, P., Mueller, G., & Havel, E. (2002). Life on the "outs"—examination of the facility to community transition of incarcerated youth. *Exceptional Children, 69*(1), 7–22.

Burke, M. D., Hagan, S. L., & Grossen, B. (1998). What curriculum designs and strategies accommodate diverse learners. *Teaching Exceptional Children, 31*(1), 34–38.

Calabrese, R. L., & Barton, A. M. (1994). Teaching students to be part of a democratic society. *Education Digest, 59*(8), 54–58.

Cottle, T. J. (1976). *Barred from school—2 million children.* Washington, DC: The New Republic Book Company.

Daniels, V. I. (1998, March/April). How to manage disruptive behavior in inclusive classrooms. *Teaching Exceptional Children, 30,* 26–31.

Deshler, D. D., & Shumaker, J. B. (1986). Learning strategies: An instructional alternative to low achieving adolescents. *Exceptional Children, 52*(6), 583–589.

Diamond, M., & Hopson, J. (1998). *The magic trees of the mind: How to nurture your child's intelligence, creativity and healthy emotions from birth through adolescence.* New York: Dutton.

Elliot, S. N. (1993). *Caring to learn: A report on the positive impact of a caring curriculum.* Greenfield, MA: The Northeast Foundation for Children.

Farrell, E. E. (1908–1909). Special classes in the New York City schools. *Journal of Psycho-Aesthetics, 13*, 91.

Gardner, H. (1993). *Multiple intelligences: The theory in practice.* New York: Basic Books.

Gartner, A., & Lipsky, D. K. (1999). Inclusion and school restructuring: A new synergy. In R. A. Villa, J. S. Thousand, W. Stainback, & S. Stainback (Eds.), *Restructuring for caring and effective education* (2nd ed., pp. 23–53). Baltimore: Brookes Publishing.

Giangreco, M. F., Edelman, S., Cloniger, C., & Dennis, R. (1992). My child has a classmate with severe disabilities: What parents of nondisabled children think about full inclusion. *Developmental Disabilities Bulletin, 20*(2), 1–12.

Gillies, R., & Ashman, A. F. (2000). The effects of cooperative learning on students with learning difficulties in the lower elementary school. *The Journal of Special Education, 34*(10), 19–27.

Goleman, D. (1995). *Emotional intelligence. Why it can matter more than IQ.* New York: Bantam Books.

Greenwood, C. R. (1991). Longitudinal analysis of time, engagement, and achievement in at-risk versus nonrisk students. *Exceptional Children, 57*, 521–535.

Hall, C. Z., Lindzey, G., & Campbell, J. B. (1998). *Theories of personality* (4th ed.). New York: John Wiley & Sons.

Hammeken, P. A. (2000). *Inclusion: 450 strategies for success: A practical guide for all educators who teach students with disabilities.* Minnetonka, MI: Peytral Publications.

Harvard Education Letter (1996). *Changing the way we think about kids with disabilities: A conversation with Tom Hehir.* Cambridge, MA: Author.

Hayward, E. (2002, July 2). MCAS gains show gaps. *The Boston Herald,* p. 3.

Hendrickson, J. M., Shokoohi-Yekta, M., Hamre-Nietupski, S., & Gable, R. (1996). Middle and high school students' perceptions on being friends with peers with severe disabilities. *Exceptional Children, 63,*19–28.

Henley, M., & Long, N.J. (1999). Teaching emotional intelligence to impulsive-aggressive youth. *Reclaiming Children and Youth: Journal of Emotional and Behavioral Problems, 7*(4), 224–229.

Henley, M. (2003). *Teaching self-control: A curriculum for responsible behavior* (2nd ed.). Bloomington, IN: National Educational Service.

Janney, R. E., Snell, M. E., Beers, M. K., & Raynes, M. (1995). Integrating students with moderate and severe disabilities into general education classes. *Exceptional Children, 61*(5), 425–439.

Johnson, D. W., & Johnson, R. T. (1986). Mainstreaming and cooperative learning strategies. *Exceptional Children , 52*(6), 553–561.

Johnson, L. J., & Pugach, M. C. (1995). Unlocking expertise among classroom teachers through structured dialogue: Extending research on peer collaboration. *Exceptional Children, 62*, 101–110.

Klinger, J. K., Vaughn, S., Schumm, J., Cohen, F., & Forgan, J. (1998). Inclusion or pull-out: Which do students prefer? *Journal of Learning Disabilities, 31*, 148–158.

Knitzer, J., Steinberg, Z., & Fleisch, B. (1990). *At the schoolhouse door: An examination of programs and policies for children with behavioral and emotional problems.* New York: Bank Street College of Education.

Kohn, A. (1997). The limits of teaching skills. *Reaching Today's Youth: The Community Circle of Caring Journal, 1*(4), 14–16.

Langdon, C. A. (1996). The third annual Phi Delta Kappan poll of teachers' attitudes towards public schools. *Phi Delta Kappan, 3*(78), 244–250.

Lanier, N. J., & Lanier, W. L. (1996). The effects of experience on teachers' attitudes toward incorporating special education students into the regular classroom. *Education, 117*, 234–237.

Lewin, K. (1936). *Principles of topical psychology.* New York: McGraw-Hill.

Long, N. J., & Morse, W. C. (1996). *Conflict in the classroom: The education of at-risk and troubled youth* (5th ed.). Austin, TX: Pro-Ed.

Marino, S. B., Miller, R., & Monahan, R. G. (1996). Teacher attitudes toward inclusion: Implications for teacher education schools in 2000. *Education, 117*, 316–321.

Marzano, R. J. (2003). *What works in schools: Translating research into action.* Alexandria, VA: Association for Supervision and Curriculum Development.

Maslow, A. H. (1970). *Motivation and personality* (2nd ed.). New York: Harper and Row.

McGregor, G., & Vogelsberg, R. T. (1998). *Inclusive schooling practices: Pedagogical research foundations.* Baltimore: Brookes Publishing.

McLesky, J., & Waldron, N. L. (1996). Responses to questions teachers and administrators frequently ask about inclusive school programs. *Phi Delta Kappan, 78*(2), 150–156.

Mendler, A. (2000). *Motivating students who don't care.* Bloomington, IN: National Educational Service.

Miller, E. (1996). Changing the way we think about kids with disabilities: A conversation with Tom Hehir. *Harvard Education Letter, 10*(4), 5–7.

Monda-Amaya, L., & Pavri, S. (2001). Social support in inclusive schools: Student and teacher perspectives. *Exceptional Children, 67*(3), 391–411.

Murphy, F. V. (2003). *Making inclusion work: A practical guide for teachers.* Norwood, MA: Christopher-Gordon Publishers, Inc.

Myles, B. S., & Simpson, R. L. (1989). Regular educators' modification preferences for mainstreaming mildly handicapped students. *Journal of Special Education, 22*, 479–491.

Phi Delta Kappa Commission on Discipline (1982). *Handbook for developing schools with good discipline.* Bloomington, IN: Phi Delta Kappa.

Redl, F., & Wineman, D. (1952). *Controls from within.* Glencoe, IL: The Free Press.

Reynolds, M. C., Wang, M. C., & Walberg, H. J. (1998). Categorical programs. LSS Publication Series No. 98-18. Retrieved February 13, 2002 from http://www.temple.edu/LSS/pub98-18.htm.

Ritter, D. R. (1989). Teachers' perceptions of problem behavior in general and special education. *Exceptional Children, 55*, 559–565.

Rosenthal, R., & Jacobsen, L. (1968). *Pygmalion in the classroom: Teacher expectations and pupils' intellectual development.* New York: Holt, Rinehart, and Winston.

Rutherford, R. B., Mathur, S. R., & Quinn, M. (1998). Promoting social communication skills through cooperative learning and direct instruction. *Education and Treatment of Children, 21*(3), 354–361.

Sealander, K. A. (1999). *Collaboration for success: Simple instructional strategies for the classroom.* Retrieved February 13, 2002 from http://www. indiana.edu/~div 16/feature.htm.

Smith, S. (1979). *No easy answers: The learning disabled child at home and at school.* New York: Bantam Books.

Smith, S. (1988). The lab school of Washington. *Pointer, 32*(3), 5–7.

Stainback, S., & Stainback, W. (1990). Inclusive schooling. In W. Stainback & S. Stainback (Eds.). *Support networks for inclusive schooling* (pp. 3–24). Baltimore: Brookes Publishing.

Staub, D., & Peck, C. A. (1994). What are the outcomes for nondisabled students? *Educational Leadership, 52*(4), 36–40.

Steinbeck, J. (1952). *East of Eden.* New York: Viking Press.

Sylwester, R. (2000). *A biological brain in a cultural classroom: Applying biological research to classroom management.* Thousand Oaks, CA: Corwin Press.

Taylor, S. J., & Searl, S. J. (1987). The disabled in America: History, policy and trends. In P. Knoblock (Ed.), *Understanding exceptional children and youth* (pp. 5–68). Boston: Little, Brown and Company.

The Responsive Classroom (n.d.). *About the Responsive Classroom: Principles and practices.* Retrieved June 5, 2003, from http://www.responsiveclassroom.org/Rcinfo.htm

The Task Force on Children Out of School (1970). *The way we go to school.* Boston, MA: Author.

U.S. Department of Commerce (December, 1997). Disabilities affect one-fifth of all Americans: Proportion could increase in coming decade. *Census Brief* #CENBR/97-5.

U.S. Department of Education (1999). Twenty-first annual report to Congress on the implementation of the Individuals with Disabilities Education Act. Washington, DC: U.S. Government Printing Office.

U.S. Department of Education (2000). *Twenty-second annual report to Congress on the implementation of the Individuals with Disabilities Education Act.* Washington, DC: U.S. Government Printing Office.

U.S. Department of Education (2001). *Twenty-third annual report to Congress on the implementation of the Individuals with Disabilities Education Act.* Washington, DC: U.S. Government Printing Office.

U.S. Department of Education (2002). Twenty-fourth annual report to Congress on the implementation of the Individuals with Disabilities Education Act. Washington, DC: U.S. Government Printing Office.

Wagner, M., Blackorby, J., Cameto, R., & Newman, L. (1993). *What makes a difference? Influences on post-school outcomes of youth with disabilties.* Menlo Park, CA: SRI International.

Wasta, S., Scott, M.G., Marchand-Martella, N., & Harris, R. (1999). From the great wall to an inclusive classroom—Integrated instruction at work. *Teaching Exceptional Children, 31*(6), 60–65.

Wenz-Gross, M., & Siperstain, G. N. (1998). Students with learning problems at risk in middle school: Stress, social support, and adjustment. *Exceptional Children, 65,* 91–100.

Zigmond, N., & Miller, S. E. (1986). Assessment for instructional planning. *Exceptional Children, 52*(6), 501–509.

Zylstra, E. (2001). A year with Bobby. *Educational Leadership, 59*(3), 74–75.

About the Author

MARTIN HENLEY, PH.D., is a professor in the Education Department at Westfield State College and director of Pegasus Center for Education. He is a Vietnam veteran. After his war service, he was awarded two fellowships to Syracuse University where he earned an M.A. in special education with an emphasis in urban education and a Ph.D. in special education with an emphasis on students with emotional and behavioral disorders. His public school teaching career included positions in inner-city elementary schools and in special education. He has served as a Head Start director and a principal of Jowonio, an inclusive school for students with autism and serious emotional problems.

In addition to his teaching duties at Westfield State College, Dr. Henley has held various administrative positions. He has been coordinator of special education undergraduate programs, director of graduate and continuing education special education programs, and chairman of the undergraduate college honors program. Dr. Henley is a frequent presenter at professional conferences and has published numerous articles on school discipline and violence prevention. He co-authored *Teaching Students With Mild Disabilities* with Roberta Ramsey and Robert Algozzine. Other books include *Teaching Self-Control: A Curriculum for Responsible Behavior.*

Dr. Henley lives in Westfield, Massachusetts with his wife, Teresa, daughter, Maggie, and dog, Daisy. He is an avid runner and golfer.

About *Creating Successful Inclusion Programs* and the National Educational Service

The mission of the National Educational Service is to provide tested and proven resources that help those who work with youth create safe and caring schools, agencies, and communities where all children succeed. *Creating Successful Inclusion Programs: Guidelines for Teachers and Administrators* is just one of many resources and staff development opportunities NES provides that focus on building a community circle of caring. If you have any questions, comments, or manuscripts you would like us to consider for publication, please contact us at the address below. Or visit our Web site at:

www.nesonline.com

Staff Development Opportunities Include:

Improving Schools Through Quality Leadership
Integrating Technology Effectively
Creating Professional Learning Communities
Building Cultural Bridges
Discipline With Dignity
Ensuring Safe Schools
Managing Disruptive Behavior
Reclaiming Youth at Risk
Working With Today's Families

National Educational Service
304 W. Kirkwood Avenue, Suite 2
Bloomington, IN 47404-5132
(812) 336-7700
(800) 733-6786 (toll-free number)
FAX (812) 336-7790
e-mail: nes@nesonline.com
www.nesonline.com

NEED MORE COPIES OR ADDITIONAL RESOURCES ON THIS TOPIC?

Need more copies of this book? Want your own copy? Need additional resources on this topic? If so, you can order additional materials by using this form or by calling us toll free at (800) 733-6786 or (812) 336-7700. Or you can order by FAX at (812) 336-7790, or visit our website at www.nesonline.com.

Title	Price*	Quantity	Total
Creating Successful Inclusion Programs	$ 9.95		
Building Classroom Communities	9.95		
Anger Management for Youth	24.95		
Adventure Education for the Classroom Community	89.00		
Discipline with Dignity for Challenging Youth	24.95		
Motivating Students Who Don't Care	9.95		
Reclaiming Youth At Risk	23.95		
Teaching Self-Control	27.95		
Teasing and Harassment	9.95		
The Bullying Prevention Handbook	23.95		
		SUBTOTAL	
		SHIPPING	
Continental U.S.: Please add 6% of order total. Outside continental U.S.: Please add 8% of order total.			
		HANDLING	
Continental U.S.: Please add $4. Outside continental U.S.: Please add $6.			
		TOTAL (U.S. funds)	

*Price subject to change without notice.

❑ Check enclosed   ❑ Purchase order enclosed
❑ Money order   ❑ VISA, MasterCard, Discover, or American Express (circle one)

Credit Card No._____ Exp. Date_____
Cardholder Signature _____

SHIP TO:
First Name_____ Last Name_____
Position _____
Institution Name _____
Address _____
City_____ State_____ ZIP _____
Phone_____ FAX_____
E-mail _____

National Educational Service
304 West Kirkwood Avenue, Suite 2
Bloomington, IN 47404-5132
(812) 336-7700 • (800) 733-6786 (toll-free number)
FAX (812) 336-7790
e-mail: nes@nesonline.com • www.nesonline.com